Royal Academy of Arts Cookery Book

A collection of recipes, illustrations and thoughts on
food by present Members and staff of the Royal Academy,
researched and compiled by Constance-Anne Parker.

The Royal Academy is grateful to its
Members and also in many cases to their
wives for their help and for their contributions
to this Cookery Book.

The recipes have been edited by
Caroline Conran and we are grateful to her for the
help and time which she has so generously
contributed to this book.
Cover "The Chef At The Hotel Chatham"
by William Orpen R.A.
Section pages illustrated by John Ward R.A.
"Noshtalgia" illustrations by Elizabeth Blackadder R.A.
Index illustrations by Christopher Sanders R.A.
Advisory Editor Margaret Casson.
The contents of this book have been
collated by Selina Fellows assisted by Marie Valsimidi
and Lesley Woodbridge.

Designed and produced by
David Pocknell's Company Limited.
ISBN 0 900946 30 X
©Royal Academy of Arts, London 1981.
Printed and bound in Spain
by TONSA, San Sebastian
Déposito Legal: S.S. 446 - 1981

Contents

Foreword

Nobody in Burlington House is less qualified than I am to introduce a Cookery Book. Although as a Boy Scout I won a badge for cooking, the taste for it seems to have left me. I am never seen in the kitchen except to wash up. I shop (if compelled) only in supermarkets. I've never even opened, much less consulted, a good food guide and although I dislike bad food as much as anyone I do not strive very hard, I'm ashamed to say, in search of better.

How different from my colleagues, happily sniffing, sipping, fingering, tasting and eventually eating and drinking their leisurely way through one delicous recipe after another in search of their perfect (and thus their favourite) dish. Generously they have invited us to share their pleasure by letting us into the secret of what it all is and how it's all done, plus the extra seasoning of illustrations.

We all hope you enjoy the results as much as the cooks quite obviously have enjoyed the preparations.

Sir Hugh Casson
President of the Royal Academy of Arts

Introduction

It is a tradition – nurtured largely perhaps by Trilby and La Boheme – that artists spend their lives either starving in garrets or roistering in cafés and bars.

The truth, as always, lies between. Artists are certainly nearly always poor and often forced to be frugal, but like all those who cultivate and respond to their senses they have always enjoyed good food and drink and convivial company, and there are plenty of records in word and paint to prove it. In the mid seventeenth century, when Van Dyck settled in Britain, he developed the practice of inviting artists and connoisseurs to dine at his home and similar gatherings have long continued in other painters' houses and at various hosteleries. More formally, artists dined annually at the Foundling Hospital in London from 1746 and it was at such a dinner, in 1759, that the idea of a society of artists arose and this was the forerunner of the Royal Academy of Arts, founded in 1768.

The first President, Sir Joshua Reynolds, regularly had guests to breakfast and, at dinners, did not hesitate to criticise things which were not quite right – "A good wine," he remarked, "but not yet fit for drinking" and, when on one occasion the peas were overcooked and yellow, said "Take them to Hammersmith" and, when asked why, replied "It's the way to Turnham Green."

Although the Royal Academy Dining Club has met regularly since its founding in 1813, the grandest celebration at table is the Royal Academy Banquet, held practically every year since 1770, to mark the opening of the Summer Exhibition.

"See now the grandest glory of the year
When to his board the Painter bids the Peer,
Where Poets, Statesmen, Soldiers, Bishops rush
To bow before the triumph of the brush.
Where even Princes play the honoured part
Before the Great Nobility of Art
The most resplendent Dinner of the year
For England's genius assembles here
The Painter's table is by none outvied,
Which make the humblest dauber flush with pride."
from *"A Rap at the R.A., 1875"*

On this great and notable occasion the Members sit down to dine with nearly 200 distinguished guests in the Great Gallery III. There is less formality today, fewer speeches and the menu is not nearly so lavish as it used to be. Here is an example of a Victorian menu:

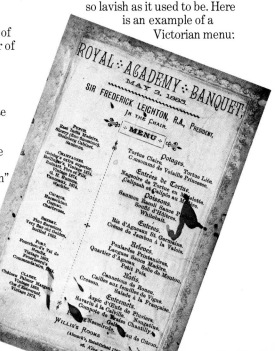

In 1815 there was a near catastrophe. Sir Walter Scott, one of the guests that year, describes it in a letter: "You may have seen at Somerset House an immense bronze chandelier with several hundred burners weighing three or four tons at least. On the day previous to the public exhibition of the paintings, the Royal Academicians are in use, as your Lordship knows, to give an immensely large dinner party to people of distinction, supposed to be amateurs of the art, to literary men, to amateurs in general, and the Lord knows whom besides. I happened to be there the first time this ponderous mass of bronze was suspended. Beneath it was placed a large table, or tier of tables, rising above each other like the shelves of a dumb waiter, and furnished with as many glasses, tumblers, decanters and so forth, as might have set up an entire glass shop – the numbers of the company – upwards of 150 persons – requiring such a supply.

Old West presided, and was supported by Jockey of Norfolk on the one side and by one of the Royal Dukes on the other. We had just drunk a preliminary toast or two when – the Lord preserve us! – a noise was heard like that which precedes an earthquake – the links of the massive chain by which this beastly lump of bronze was suspended, began to give way, and the mass descending slowly encountered the table beneath, which was positively annihilated by the pressure, the whole of the glass ware being at once destroyed. What was very odd, the chain, after this manifestation of weakness, continued to hold fast; and we, I think to

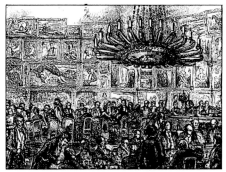

the credit of our courage, continued our sitting. Had it really given way – as the architecture of Somerset House has in general been deemed unsubstantial – it must have broke the floor like a bombshell and carried us all down to the cellars of that great national edifice. A fine paragraph we should have made!"

In this century probably the best remembered Banquets are those of 1949 when the then President, Sir Alfred Munnings, made his notoriously contentious remarks about Picasso and Matisse, and of 1967 when Lady Violet Bonham Carter, Baroness Asquith replying for "The Guests" made R.A. history with a brilliant speech that celebrated the first time in nearly 200 years that women had been invited to be present.

In the following pages, which in most cases were the result of taped discussions, the Members accompany their recipes with personal comment upon different attitudes to food and drink these are complemented by similar anecdotes from the past.

SOUPS

Edward Bawden

R.A. 1956

Born 1903. Studied Cambridge School of Art and R.C.A. under Paul Nash. War Artist visiting France, Yugoslavia, Sudan, Ethiopia, Eritrea, Palestine, Syria, Iraq and Iran. Teaching at Goldsmith's College and R.C.A. since 1930. C.B.E. 1946

Yes, I do cook for myself. I've been a widower for 11 years but before that in my married days my wife wouldn't let me go into the kitchen and if she did give me some job to do, I never did it properly – except washing up, I'm quite good at that. But then when I lived alone I had to do something about cooking. I'm not a good cook. If I'm cooking for myself I don't take much trouble. If I have visitors, as I very often do, then I take time and trouble. How did I learn to cook? Well, as soon as you become a widower you suddenly find, to your astonishment, that you are ringed round by women! So I have a large circle of friends from whom I can ask advice. I taught myself by reading recipes and by experiment – and by throwing a lot in the dustbin!

I'm more or less a vegetarian, but I have a "visiting" cat and we both like fish, so we have it fairly often, at least once a week.

If it is necessary to have a meal out, I would choose an Indian or Italian restaurant for preference.

I have illustrated a dozen cookery books, most of them as a young man when I was seeking work from publishers. Food is not a major interest of mine, if it comes to spending money, I'd rather spend it on a book.

Mushroom Soup

Serves 4

¾ lb mushrooms

2 oz butter

Garlic, parsley, nutmeg

A thick slice of bread

1¾ pints stock

3 to 4 ozs cream

Seasoning

Wash mushrooms: do not peel or remove stalks. Melt butter, put in mushrooms and let them soften: when moisture starts to run add a small piece of garlic, a tablespoon of chopped parsley, salt, pepper, nutmeg and let the mushroom stew for several minutes.

Take a thick slice of crustless bread, which should have been soaked in a little of the stock: squeeze out the moisture and add to the mushrooms. Stir till the bread amalgamates with the mushrooms. Add stock and cook for 15 minutes. Liquidise. Return to a clean saucepan and when hot add boiling cream and another tablespoonful of parsley, chopped fine.

The Brick House Garden Party line drawing from "Good Food" by Ambrose Heath by permission of Faber & Faber Limited. The party consists of Eric Ravilious and Tom Hennell on the left and Edward Bawden and Tirzah Ravilious on the right.

Gertrude Hermes

R.A. 1971

Sculptor; wood engraver; teacher wood engraving R.A. Schools. Studied: Leon
Underwood's School, London. Portrait Sculpture and decorative carving for buildings;
fountain and door furniture, Shakespeare Memorial Theatre; Britannia Window,
British Pavilion, Paris, 1937.

I do cook but I'm not very good. No, I don't look upon it as a bore, I quite enjoy it when I do it and when I've asked people in. I think cooking is creative but I'm afraid I'm not very creative about it.

I don't entertain very much now, I'm getting too old! Really it's only hitting me now, my legs feel it, they are going to bits rather. If I were giving a dinner party it would probably be fillet of beef, spinach and potatoes, delicious gravy and ice cream and fruit and red wine.

I always have coffee, a piece of toast and marmalade or honey for breakfast. My favourite recipes? Oh well – Dover sole off the bone fried in butter with new potatoes and hot chicory and little mushrooms. I'd have Vichyssoise to start with and fresh lichees and cream to finish. Wine – white, Liebfraumilch preferably.

Crème Vichyssoise

2 oz butter	
3 large leeks (white part only) sliced	
1 onion chopped	
½ lb potatoes peeled and sliced	
1½ pints chicken stock	
¼ pint milk	
½ pint single cream	
Salt and pepper	
Chopped chives	

Fry leeks and onion in butter till soft but not brown. Add potatoes, stock, salt and pepper. Simmer till tender (30 mins). Cool, sieve, stir in cream, thin with milk.

Serve well chilled sprinkled with chopped chives.

Sir Hugh Casson

R.A. 1970

Born: 1910. Studied: St John's College, Cambridge, University College, London. Private practice as an architect since 1937. Prof. of Environmental Design R.C.A. 1953–75. President of R.A. since 1976. K.C.V.O. 1978.

Nobody could call me an epicure. Nevertheless the food I like I enjoy – simple rather than exotic and not too much at a time. I dislike rich food and if dragged unwillingly to a restaurant I prefer Italian cooking to French. At home by ourselves I enjoy most what amounts almost to an invalid diet – grilled fish, egg dishes, rice pudding and (to rev it up a bit) school food – deliciously cooked of course – sausages, treacle tart, baked potatoes and a great variety of soups. But I can equally enjoy the more adventurous menus devised for visiting friends by my wife to both suit me and delight them.

Eliza Acton's Apple Soup

In 1845, Eliza Acton published her 'Modern Cookery', the first important English cookery book. It included this recipe for a tart apple soup which was apparently well known in Mediaeval Britain.

Ingredients (for 6)
2 pints beef or mutton stock
1 lb cooking apples
½ level tsp of ground ginger
Salt & black pepper
4 rounded tblsp long-grain rice

Remove all fat from the surface of the prepared cool stock. Wash the apples and chop them roughly, without removing peel or core. Bring the stock to the boil in a large pan, add the apples and cover the pan with a lid. Simmer the soup over low heat until the apples are tender.

Pour the pulp through a seive, rubbing through as much as possible of the fruit pulp. Stir in the ginger and season with salt and ground pepper and re-heat.

While the soup is cooking (it should take about 30 minutes), boil the rice in plenty of salted water. Drain thoroughly through a seive and keep the rice warm. Spoon the soup into bowls, and serve the rice separately.

Maxwell Fry

R.A. 1972

Born 1899. An architect for fifty years and a landscape painter for the rest.
Was a leading figure in the English modern architectural movement in the 30's and
with wife and partner Jane Drew did a repeat performance for the tropics with work
in West Africa, Persia, India and Mauritius. Royal Gold Medal for architecture 1964.
C.B.E. 1953.

I "take part" in cooking, that is to say, I peel things! Apples and onions and I rush into the kitchen and turn the cooker down when I'm told to, to keep things simmering, I'm a sort of "Cook's Labourer."

I have an elaborate breakfast, often in bed, now. Orange juice, mixed grill, sausages and mushrooms; fried apple or banana with the bacon is very good, and toast and homemade marmalade and coffee – that's all after early morning tea! A good basis for the day. Then we have a good hot lunch, after that we tail off a bit.

We entertain in quite a big way; we had eight to lunch yesterday, we gave them salmon, red cabbage with nutmeg and apples, shoulder of lamb and

vegetables and a huge marmalade tart and then cheese. We make a lot of wine, elderflower and one from red cabbage and apples that tastes like red currants and

nettlebeer. We make lots of jellies from all the berries. We have a large garden and we grow 40 different kinds of vegetables. We have almost as much in the garden now in winter as in summer, and we keep two hives of bees. So we have our own honey. Our cooking is very budget orientated. For a treat, we'd have duck with a good orange sauce. My favourite pudding is Jane's bread and butter pudding made with marmalade. She makes lots of tarts too. We have a huge freezer which Jennie Lee gave us. It's a bit vast and to find out what's at the bottom you have to put gloves and a fur cap on before you dig. We bought that book "Food for Free" and we've tried a lot of the recipes. They are very good. We use all the different kinds of wild mushrooms and things now.

Artichoke Soup

2 lb Jerusalem artichokes
2 onions
½ oz butter
½ pint velouté sauce

Slice onions and soften in butter.
Clean artichokes and parboil in salted water then skin them. Boil till soft. Add softened onions and a little velouté sauce and put into the blender.

Dr. Samuel Johnson
(1709-84), the great lexicographer and the Academy's
first professor of Ancient Literature, seems to have
been abstemious in regard to alcohol but somewhat
over-indulgent with sauces. "After ten years'
forbearance of every fluid except tea and sherbet,"
he said, "I drank a glass of wine to the health of Sir
Joshua Reynolds on the evening of the day on which
he was knighted." His friend Mrs. Thrale recorded "His
notions of a good dinner are nothing less then delicate
– a Leg of Pork boyl'd till it drops from the bone,
almost. Veal Pye with Plumbs and Sugar and the
outside Cut of a Buttock of Beef were his favourite
Dainties, though he loves made dishes, soups etc.
Sowces his Plumb Pudden with melted Butter and
pours enough sauce into every Plate to drown all
Taste of the Victuals."

Raymond Cowern

R.A. 1968

Born 1913. Painter, etcher and draughtsman. Studied: Central School, Birmingham; RCA, London. Worked with Sakkarah Expedition of Oriental Institute of Chicago. Rome scholar of engraving 1937-39. Commissioned by Pilgrim Trust Scheme for recording Britain.

Food is for me a pleasure which, as studio adjoins kitchen – a most convenient arrangement – can begin with the smells; my sole contribution being anticipation and appreciation.

Of the art of cookery I know nothing. It is said of the Renaissance painter Piero di Cosimo that, being afraid of fire, he would hard boil fifty eggs at a time. That I could do.

If I crack an egg it's to paint with, emulsified with thick oil and varnish and water: the cookery of art so to speak. A recipe must be in plain terms e.g. "..mix to the consistency of stopping-out varnish."

My wife claims that she is no cook; that her dishes succeed or no as may studies in a sketch book. Be that as it may we enjoy them, relishing especially the fresh fish which is plentiful with us, plainly cooked and served with a delicate sauce. A bonus is stock for the Greek soup Avgolemono, a simple dish and worthy to grace any table.

Avgolemono – Greek Soup

2 pints of fish or chicken stock
2 oz rice
2 eggs
Juice of a lemon
Dessertspoon of coldwater

To stock add rice and boil till well cooked. In a basin beat up eggs till frothy, add the lemon juice and water. To this mixture add some of the hot broth spoon by spoon, stirring all the time. Pour this into the rest of the stock and stir for a few minutes over a very low heat. Season. Serve at once.

Sydney Harpley

R.A. 1981

Born 1927. Studied: R.C.A.; Hammersmith College of Art; ARCA.
Realist sculptor, portraits and figure. Sculpture in collections:
USA, New Zealand, South Africa, London, Geneva.

I think cooking should be creative, it's all a matter of taking a basic recipe and changing it according to what you've got in the cupboard. You have to be inventive – try putting marmalade in the stew. You won't taste the marmalade but you'll get the fruitiness and the sweetness. The secret is not to use too much of any ingredient so that no one flavour dominates another.

We share the cooking so I often cook. My cooking used to be "plain English" lots of stodge and suet pudding. Now I use garlic and spices, though I still like rice pudding.

We do eat out regularly, usually French, Indian and Chinese. My wife dislikes the idea of eating rabbit. Once when we were in France, we went to a restaurant and she had Coq au Vin and I had Lapin Provençal. We'd nearly finished when I said "It's funny, this rabbit had a wing!" and my wife said "Oh, my God, I've eaten bunny!" Both dishes looked very much alike, cooked in sauce and they'd mixed up the order.

We usually entertain at home, we like the intimacy of eating at home.

My wife has a marvellous chocolate mousse, absolutely superb. She spares neither time nor money on it, but it is well worth it. I make a version of mulligatawny soup, but I really have to go through the motions of making it, a little bit of this and bit of that – Indian spices, except the hot chillies. I'll have to make it and write down what I do, then you can have it.

Mulligatawny Soup

(four servings)	
1 level tsp turmeric	1 clove garlic (crushed)
1 level tsp cumin	1½ pints water
Ground black pepper to taste	
1 chicken carcass	
1 chicken stock cube	
2 medium size onions (cut up)	
1 dessertspoon tomato paste	

Mix Turmeric, Cumin, Ground Black Pepper in a little cold water and put with other ingredients into large saucepan. Bring to the boil and simmer gently for one hour. Do not add salt, as there is usually enough in the stock cube.

Sieve before serving.

Convenience Tomato Soup

1 tin of tomatoes

1 oz of butter

2 onions

1 tblsp of tomato purée

Clove of garlic

Black pepper and salt

1 tsp of caster sugar

Bay leaf

½ handful of cooked rice

1½ pints of stock

Freshly grated parmesan cheese

1 tsp of chopped parsley

Melt butter and lightly brown sliced onions, add tomato purée, finely chopped garlic, seasoning, sugar and bay leaf. Add to the stock with the tin of tomatoes. Add the pre-cooked rice and simmer for about 15 minutes – do not boil.

Serve with parmesan cheese and chopped parsley.

Ben Levene A.R.A.

Leek and Potato Soup

4 leeks

3 small potatoes

1 pint good chicken stock

2 oz butter

½ pint milk

My best soup is leek and potato.

Sizzle leeks in butter for 5 minutes then add stock and diced potatoes and simmer until tender. Put through a blender and season to taste. Add milk when heating up the soup, but if it is not to be used all at once I add the milk separately each day of re-heating.

Olwyn Bowey R.A.

Cucumber Mint Soup

Cucumbers

Mint

Flour

2 pints chicken stock

Dice cucumbers, then sweat in marge, adding lots of mint. Put on lid of pan and shake about, (add flour now if you want it thick). Gradually add chicken stock. Go on like that and when everything is soft, either sieve it, or eat it as it is. (Katy thinks the latter course infinitely preferable and she calls it the Bois de Boulogne.)

Griselda Hamilton-Baillie
ASSISTANT SECRETARY (PUBLIC RELATIONS)

Stilton Soup

1 medium sized onion

2 sticks of celery

2 oz of butter

1½ oz of flour

2½ fl oz white wine

2 pints white stock (chicken)

½ pint milk

½ lb grated Stilton cheese

2 tblsp cream

Salt and pepper (croutons)

N.B. This soup can be served chilled.

Finely chop the onion and celery and soften in butter over a gentle heat. Add flour and cook for about a minute.

Take off the heat and stir in the wine and stock. Return to the heat and bring to the boil slowly, stir continously until the soup thickens. Simmer for 25 minutes.

Add the milk and simmer for a further 2 minutes. Remove from the heat and whisk in the Stilton.

Add the cream and salt and pepper.

Sian Morgan
PUBLICATIONS DEPARTMENT

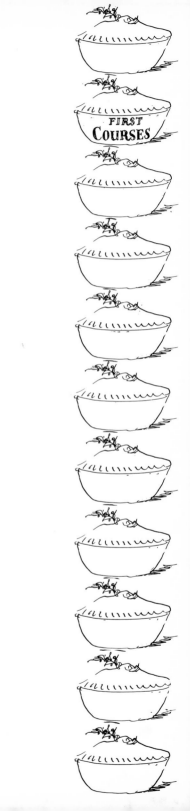

FIRST
COURSES

Anthony Whishaw

A.R.A. 1980

Born: 1930. Studied: Chelsea School Art; RCA. Won numerous prizes and Abbey Minor
Scholarship and Spanish Govt. Scholarship. Exhibited in several galleries and works
represented in various collections: Britain, Brazil, Australia, USA.
Gallery: Nicola Jacobs.

I enjoy food but frying an egg with garlic is about the limit of my cooking: When I had a scholarship to Spain I had to cook dried blood and lung! It was the cheapest thing you could get there. It came in a chunk and you fried it with onions and garlic, a bit like liver. The taste lingered on after you'd eaten it and was quite disgusting. I love some of their food but it varies a lot, it's best in the North. In the South they kill and cook their chickens so quickly that they are still suffering from rigor mortis and are very tough! But in the bars they have a custom of serving very imaginative snacks called 'Tapas' with the drinks.

I never have breakfast, but when I get to my cold studio in Wapping, I have hot marmite and for lunch usually have tuna fish and mayonnaise and rolls. My wife is a fantastic cook, very imaginative and cooks all kinds of unusual mixtures, Chinese, Spanish.

Favourite meal? Well, I like spicy foods, and really like suckling pig, but you can't get that here.

Eggs in Stilton

3 oz stilton cheese
6 eggs
3 rashers of lean bacon
6 tblsp of cream
Black pepper
A little cheddar cheese
Parsley

Put a nob of stilton cheese in the bottom of each small oven proof dish then break one raw egg into each dish. Add the rest of the stilton cheese, small pieces of fried lean bacon and cover with the cream. Top with freshly ground black pepper, a little grated cheddar cheese and some parsley. Put into moderate oven Reg 4/350 for about 20 minutes or until cheese melts.

Ralph Brown

R.A. 1972

Born: 1928. Studied: Leeds; Hammersmith and Royal College of Art and in Paris,
Greece and Italy. Sculptor in bronze. Tutor RCA. Work in Tate; Rijksmuseum, Holland;
CAS; Leeds. Public sculpture: Hatfield; Harlow; LCC Tulse Hill; Loughborough
University; Newnham College.

I work all morning, have a light lunch, work abominably in the afternoon and then work from 5 to 9. We have dinner late. I don't cook but my wife does, she's a super inventive cook. I just like to know what's going on. My mother was a good sturdy Yorkshire cook. I still remember my childhood and Thursday baking days, she made all her own bread and pies and things. Marvellous!

We had to live on snails at one time, when we were in France and were really broke. We moved into an enormous ancient and decrepit farmhouse in the Cervennes, perched up on a mountain side. We were invited to a great village barbecue about four days after we arrived and we were told that we were living in the best place for snails in the district. The whole village used to collect snails from round our farm's retaining walls. We made the mistake of asking how to cook snails and it nearly caused a riot, everyone started to argue about the best way to cook them. We've evolved this recipe from all the conflicting advice we got.

Now we live in the Cotswolds in an area where the Romans introduced the huge Helix pomatia; they are the best but the common or garden Helix aspersa is delicious and found everywhere. The time to catch them is in the evening in summer after rain, you need wellies and a bucket and a torch. You also need a box or big plastic bowl well covered with fine mesh. Snails move like whippets if they escape! Keep them three weeks without food to get rid of any toxic stuff they may have eaten. Keep in a cool dry place. The last few days fatten them on lettuce leaves and thyme or other herbs. They make a wonderful meal.

Snails Caroline

4 doz snails
250 grammes of butter
1 very large clove of garlic, crushed
1 shallot or a little onion, finely chopped
A good handful of parsley, finely chopped
25 grammes (about 1 oz) lean ham, finely chopped
25 grammes button mushrooms, finely chopped
Salt, ground black pepper

Buy live snails or collect them on a rainy day and starve them for two weeks.

To prepare Place in cold water and bring to the boil.

This way they come out of their shells as they run out of oxygen. If placed in boiling water they retreat back into their shells and are difficult to remove. This stage is best done on a camping stove or whatever, in the garden shed as the smell is rather unpleasant. Boil for 10 minutes then drain. The rest can be done indoors. Hook out each snail with a snail pick, and holding under a running cold tap remove the little black end of the coiled bit, which is the lower intestine, and rinse well. This is quicker than it sounds.

To Cook Place in cold water and white wine with salt and pepper, and a good bunch of herbs (or a couple of bags of bouquet garni).

Simmer for 50 minutes. Drain.

The Sauce This is basically the traditional garlic butter sauce used in

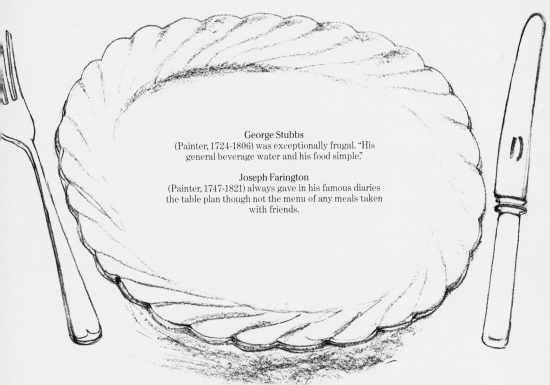

George Stubbs
(Painter, 1724-1806) was exceptionally frugal. "His
general beverage water and his food simple."

Joseph Farington
(Painter, 1747-1821) always gave in his famous diaries
the table plan though not the menu of any meals taken
with friends.

escargots Bourguignon, but when we lived down in the Cevennes my wife delighted our French friends with her minor addition of ham and mushrooms. Many of them now use this modified version, calling them escargots Caroline, so there is a tiny corner of France where the cuisine has been corrupted by the English, I think in this case for the better. Escargots Cevenots are revolting.

We find shells an awful fiddle to clean, and use fireproof snail cocottes with deep walls. We therefore proceed as follows. Barely melt the butter on a very gentle heat and stir in all the other ingredients. Remove from heat and add salt and ground black pepper to taste. Put a snail into each well of the cocotte and using a teaspoon fill to the brim with the sauce – keep stirring the pan as all the interesting bits keep sinking to the bottom. If the sauce thickens, warm it gently again. I'm sure this melting process, before the cooking proper, helps to blend the flavours. The prepared pots can now be put on one side until needed.

To serve Put in a hot oven for about 8 minutes until bubbling and browning, and serve with plenty of crusty French bread and lots of red wine – Côtes du Rhône or Côtes de Provence go well. A complete and perfect meal is 1½ or 2 dozen of these snails, followed by a long pause with more wine, finishing with a huge bowl of fresh strawberries and a glass of armagnac.

William Bowyer

R.A. 1981

R.W.S., R.P. Head of Fine Art Maidstone College of Art since 1971. Born: May 25th 1926, married 1951 Vera Mary Small. Two sons, one daughter. Educ., Burslem School of Art, Royal College of Art. Hon. Sec., New English Art Club. Recreations: Cricket (Old Meadonians Cricket Club).

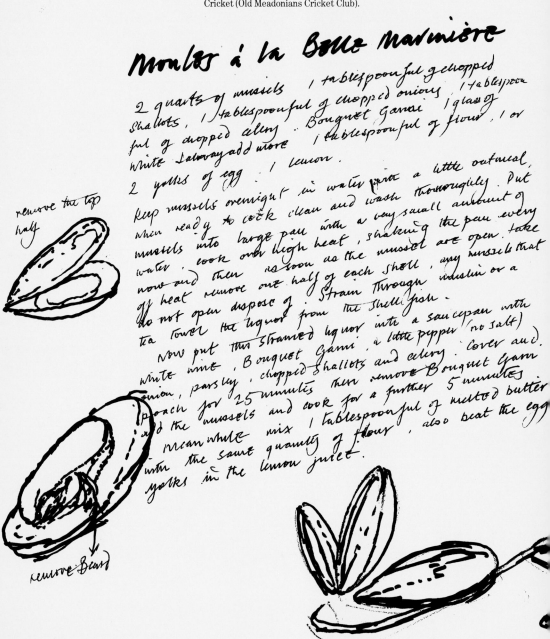

Moules à la Belle Marinière

2 quarts of mussels. 1 tablespoonful g chopped Shallots, 1 tablespoonful of chopped onions, 1 tablespoonful of chopped celery. Bouquet Garni. 1 glass of white Saloway add more. 1 tablespoonful of flour. 1 or 2 yolks of egg. 1 lemon.

Keep mussels overnight in water put a little oatmeal, when ready to cook clean and wash thoroughly. Put mussels into large pan with a very small amount of water. cook over high heat, shaking the pan every now and then. as soon as the mussel are open. take off heat remove out half of each shell, any mussels that do not open dispose of. Strain through muslin or a tea towel the liquor from the shellfish.

Now put this strained liquor into a saucepan with white wine, Bouquet Garni. a little pepper (no salt) onion, parsley, chopped shallots and celery. Cover and poach for 25 minutes then remove Bouquet Garni and the mussels and cook for a further 5 minutes meanwhile mix 1 tablespoonful of melted butter with the same quantity of flour, also beat the egg yolks in the lemon juice.

remove the top half

remove Beard

30

lift out the mussels with a skimming ladle, and put them on hot dishes. Bind the sauce with the butter and flour and beat the mixture until the roux has melted into the sauce, beating all the time. Move away from the heat and add the egg yolks treated with lemon juice. Pour this sauce over the mussels; sprinkle with chopped parsley and serve.

Ann Christopher

A.R.A. 1980

Born: 1947 – Watford, Herts. Studied: Harrow School of Art 1965/66. West of England
College of Art 1966/69 (Dip. A.D. Sculpture). Awards: Daily Telegraph "Young
Sculpture" Comp. 1971. Arts Council Grant 1973 & 1976. South West Arts Award 1976.
Exhibitions: Oxford Gallery, Oxford. Festival Gallery, Bath. J.P.L. Fine Arts, London.
'Profile', Bristol City Art Gallery. London Group Exhibitions. Collections: Contemporary
Art Society. Bristol City Art Gallery. Chantrey Collection. Commissions: Daily
Telegraph Magazine – Sculpture. Bristol Literary Dinners – Sculpture.
Lives and works near Bath.

A particularly memorable meal was totally snails, traditionally done with garlic, we had about 40 each. They were followed by a massive bowl of strawberries. I'd never tried snails before and didn't like the idea of eating them, but everyone was teasing me so much that I made myself try one, and immediately I got completely hooked.

I have pretty basic tastes otherwise. I love eating fish, any kind of fish, but specially mussels and mackerel. Apart from fish, my other big thing is vegetables, all vegetables. My greatest dislike is overcooked vegetables. I can't stand them. I boil mine very quickly.

I like to make salads. In the spring, I'll pick anything in the garden that's green and that I know isn't poisonous – except grass! I'm an obsessive eater of fresh vegetables.

When I'm working, I haven't really time to cook and then it's a chore, but when I have time to spare I quite enjoy cooking. I do like cookery books, with pictures, though the one I use most hasn't any!

I enjoy wines though I don't know much about them.

Champignons aux Escargots
(Mushrooms stuffed with snails)

32 snails – tinned	
1 glass dry white wine	
1 grated carrot	
Thyme, salt and pepper	
16 large flat mushrooms	
1 tblsp olive oil	
1 shallot	
2 cloves garlic	
1 tblsp chopped parsley	
3 oz white breadcrumbs	
A little butter	

Drain snails, rinse in warm water.

Marinate snails in wine, carrot, salt, pepper and thyme for at least ½ hr.

Remove mushroom heads, coat lightly with olive oil, salt and pepper and grill gently.

Finely chop mushroom stalks, shallot, garlic, parsley and drained snails.

Mix with breadcrumbs – moistened with a little marinade.

Put mixture into mushroom heads, dot with butter and grill for 10 – 15 mins. NB. very rich – enough for four.

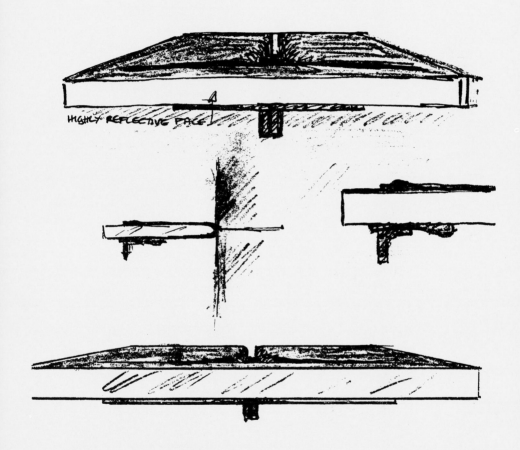

HIGHLY REFLECTIVE FACE

SAND CAST MAIN
PIECE WITH WAX/BRONZE
INNER PIECE.

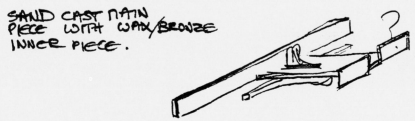

Willi Soukop

R.A. 1969

Born: 1907. Studied: Apprenticed to engraver; Vienna Academy Fine Art. Came to England, Dartington Hall, 1934. Taught at various Art Schools. Sculptures for new schools: Herts, Leics, Derbs, Staffs, LCC. Work in many private and public collections. Archibald McIndoe Award, 1964.

I have tea and bread and jam for breakfast. I can still wear the suits I had 25 years ago, so I do not add to my circumference which I think is due to my breakfast. When I first came over to England I was very homesick for Austrian dishes like Wiener Schnitzel and goulash, so I tried to make them myself. But I couldn't buy paprika in Devonshire where I was living. So at the village shop they gave me red pepper instead and I put a liberal amount into my goulash thinking that cayenne was like paprika. My whole mouth felt as if it was going up in flames. That cured me of wanting goulash, in England, anyway.

My creative cooking is when my wife is away, then I put all sorts of things together in a saucepan. Just whatever there is. Sometimes it's very good, sometimes it's appalling! It's hit or miss and I can't repeat my success. Sauerkraut, noodles and smoked ham is delicious. It may give you indigestion but, my goodness, it's a fulfilling meal! I go for Viennese meat dishes not chocolate and cream cakes. Liver dumplings are good but don't make for a slimline! When I was a little boy we used to help to make the apple strudel. The pastry had to be rolled and then we stretched it till it was paper thin. For a special meal I'd have that, with liver dumpling soup and Wiener Schintzel with potato salad. After all that I wouldn't be able to walk home!

Liver and Bacon Pâté

1 lb liver sliced	
6 rashers bacon	
¼ lb mushrooms	
Thyme	
Lemon peel	
Garlic	
Bayleaf	
Pastry	
Sherry, or port, or white wine	

Sauté the liver gently in good dripping or butter. Add the mushrooms sliced, and when they have cooked a minute or two pour into the pan whatever wine you are using and let it reduce by half.

In a small terrine, or pie-dish, put a layer of chopped bacon, then a layer of the liver mixture, seasoned with salt, pepper, a very little garlic, thyme and lemon peel, another layer of bacon, and so on until it is all used up. Cover with a crust of pastry, stand in a pan of water, and bake in a moderate oven.

This can be eaten hot or cold, and can also be done without the pastry crust, in which case cover it with a buttered paper and the lid of the terrine. *(E.D.)*

curb

WILLI SOUKOP

Kipper Pâté

1 large packet frozen raw kipper fillets

1 medium size pot cottage cheese

¼ packet Philadelphia cream cheese

1 tblsp margarine

Tabasco sauce to taste (I use 2 tsp)

Black freshly ground pepper

Juice of ½ lemon

Take the skin off the kipper fillets when defrosted – <u>do not cook</u>. Put them with all the other ingredients in a blender and blend until smooth. Chill.

Elisabeth Frink R.A.

Munkaczina

Oranges

Onion

Stoned black olives

Red pepper

Salt

Olive oil

Take one or more oranges and cut them in slices crossways. Peel the slices and remove the pips and white in the middle of the round. Arrange a bed of slices of orange at the bottom of the dish, and cover with finely chopped onion.

On the onion place a bed of stoned black olives, and sprinkle with red pepper, salt and olive oil.

Frederick Gore R.A.

Smoked Mackerel Pâté

Garlic

Smoked mackerel

Breadcrumbs

Olive oil

Pinch of salt

Milk

Mix all ingredients in the blender till it becomes a beautiful creamy white pâté. I can't give the amounts, I just judge it by eye. Very nice with sliced lemon and watercress.

Roger de Grey R.A.

Chicken Liver Pâté

1 lb chicken livers

3 tblsp chicken fat

2 diced onions

2 hard boiled eggs

Heat 2 tablespoons of fat and lightly brown the onions.

Wash and cook the livers in the remaining tablespoon of fat for ten minutes. Grind or chop liver, eggs and onions to a smooth paste and add seasoning.

Serve with brown bread – ideally rye bread. I prefer salt added afterwards when the pâté is spread on bread.

Ben Levene A.R.A.

Tuna Fish

1 tin of tuna fish

2 hard boiled eggs

2 tblsp mayonnaise

½ finely chopped onion (optional)

Sprinkling of parsley, chives, tarragon

Salt and pepper

Mash the hard boiled eggs with the mayonnaise and add the onion, herbs and seasoning.

Add to tin of tuna fish. Serve with toast.

Ben Levene A.R.A.

Peter Blake

R.A. 1981

Born: 1932. Studied: Gravesend School of Art and RCA. Exhibited: ICA; Guggenheim
Competition; Musee d'Art Moderne, Paris. Works in permanent collections: Tate;
Trinity College, Cambridge and Carlisle City Gallery. Illustrations for
Oxford Illustrated Old Testament, 1968.

My basic diet is mostly of rather plain food, but I do like the occasional excursion into the exotic dishes. Particularly Chinese or Indian. I don't care for over creative cooking, it's too rich and creamy and too many different flavours cancelling each other out.

I've always thought I might one day paint one of these Literary Breakfasts. I just have Grapefruit and toast when I'm trying to lose weight.

For 11 years we lived in the country where there was nowhere much to eat out, so now we are in London we go out quite often. We have such a tiny flat that we really have no facilities for entertaining at home, so we normally take people out. Favourite dishes? Oh, escargots, steaks, duck, knuckle of ham and beans and puddings – I love puddings! And wine with the meal, of course. We usually order the house wine.

I used to be involved with Health Foods at one time now I'd probably choose Shepherd's Pie or Steak and Kidney followed by a nice Spotted Dick with raisins.

I've been painting the retiring Rector of the Royal College and they said I could have 16 guests to a dinner party that they would give for me. They were a bit horrified by my choice of menu! Smoked Mackerel, Roast Beef, Yorkshire Pudding, Roast Potatoes, Cabbage, Peas, Spotted Dick, Custard and Ice-Cream. I should enjoy that!

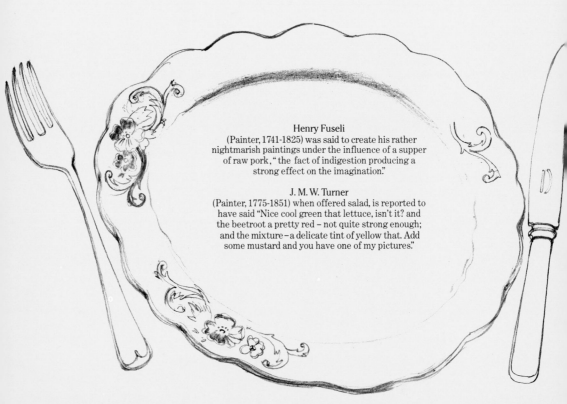

Henry Fuseli
(Painter, 1741-1825) was said to create his rather nightmarish paintings under the influence of a supper of raw pork, " the fact of indigestion producing a strong effect on the imagination."

J. M. W. Turner
(Painter, 1775-1851) when offered salad, is reported to have said "Nice cool green that lettuce, isn't it? and the beetroot a pretty red – not quite strong enough; and the mixture – a delicate tint of yellow that. Add some mustard and you have one of my pictures."

Anthony Gross

R.A. 1980

Born: 1905. Studied: Slade School; Central School, Ecole des Beaux Arts, Paris;
Escuela Real, Madrid. Official war artist 1941-1945. Taught: Slade and Central School.
Work in public collections throughout world. Illustrated: Cocteau's "Les Enfants
Terribles"; "The Forsythe Saga"; "Wuthering Heights," etc.
Collaborated with Hector Hoppin making several cartoon films.

Cooking should not be anything invented – you should stick to traditional recipes of each area in a country – keep to the way you were taught by your mother or your grandmother. Real country cooking is the best anywhere in the world and should not be altered a jot.

Cooking is one of the best things in life. I remember when I first met my wife she cooked me an entire veal liver in one piece wrapped around with strips of pork fat. It was cooked in an iron pot roast. It was beautiful! It made up my mind for me and we married soon after.

In the part of France I know best, they say that when the Moors invaded it in the 8th C. they left behind them men who had little feet and the *pastis*, a puff pastry rolled out very thinly and folded again and again with apple, rum and sugar added. It is cooked in the hearth in a brazen pot called a tourtière. Finally red hot cinders are piled on the lid making it into an oven.

We also have dried plums or prunes in South West France, the *pruneaux d'Agen* which are dried and baked over an oak fire giving them the taste of oak. These plum trees were first brought back by returning Crusaders from the Middle East in the 12th C. They are the very special *prunes d'ente*. They are most delicious when stuffed into a *real* country chicken with garlic and roasted.

My favourite dish? Oysters! True, a bad one can put you off for life. But the trick is to have them served still attached to the deep shell, then you separate it with your knife, and what HO! you swallow it! Well after a dozen or so of these and a *real* chicken with prunes and garlic and a *pastis* to finish would make an acceptable meal!

Well, you have three or four recipes above! We will leave it at that.

CALAMARIES

1½ lbs Squid

Serves 4 starter

2 Eggs

4 Tablespoons of Milk

Seasoning — flour, salt, pepper.

METHOD : Clean Squid — by removing black ink sac, tentacles and transparent cartilage (this is found inside the squid and easily removed with the fingers). Slice horizontally and place the rings of squid in cold water. Whisk eggs and milk together then dip rings and toss in seasoned flour — deep fry a few at a time until golden brown. and drain well.

SERVE :
With wedges of lemon and brown bread and butter together with a dry white wine

Hans Frenkel
ASSISTANT SECRETARY (GENERAL)

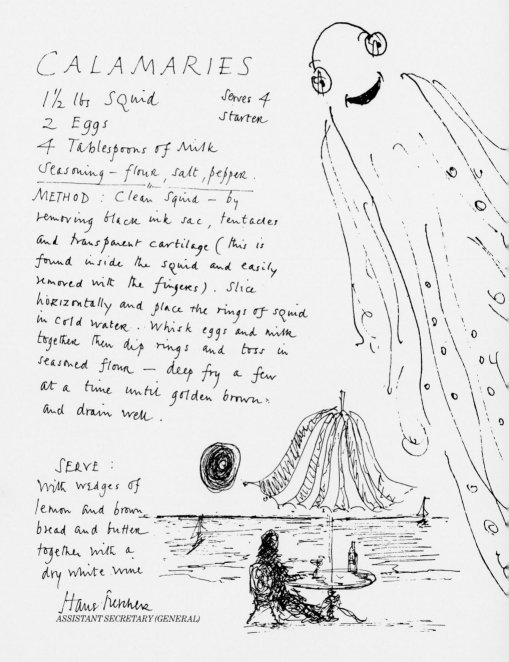

Cucumber in Sour Cream

1 large cucumber
1 small carton sour cream
1 tsp salt
1 tsp ground black pepper
1 tblsp horseradish

Peel and thinly slice cucumber. Combine sour cream, salt, pepper and horseradish. Stir together then pour over cucumber and lightly toss. Chill until ready to serve.

Debbie Godbold
FRIENDS OFFICE

Mushroom and Prawn Vinaigrette

Garlic
½ lemon
Olive oil
Salt
Black pepper
½ lb fresh mushrooms
1 lb fresh prawns
Parsley

Get a flat dish and in it make the vinaigrette, i.e. crush clove of garlic, squeeze the juice out of half a lemon, add enough olive oil, pinch of salt and plenty of freshly ground black peppercorn.

Then remove stalks from mushrooms and peel off outer skins.

Shell prawns – mix mushrooms and prawns and vinaigrette together and sprinkle with chopped parsley.

Do not refrigerate as it loses its flavour if you do.

Laura Scott
SECRETARY, ROYAL ACADEMY SCHOOLS

OEUFS EN COCOTTES avec la différence
— To serve 8 as a starter —

Skin, bone and break up the Mackerel - Line bottom of the ramekin dishes with the fish - (flatten out the fish in the dishes, otherwise the eggs will break) - then gently break an egg on top of each fish - season - Cover with single cream — Chop mushrooms finely and sprinkle over the top add small knobs of butter together with chopped parsley. Place ramekins in a pan of hot water and put in oven @ 350°/reg4 for 20 minutes until firm. It also can be served as a light luncheon, made in a soufflé dish, with salad.

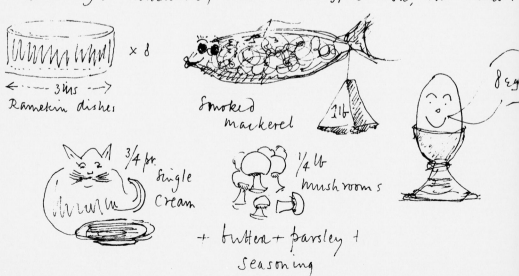

× 8

← --- 3ins ---→
Ramekin dishes

Smoked mackerel

1 lb

8 eggs

3/4 pr. single cream

1/4 lb mushrooms

+ butter + parsley + seasoning

42

MAIN COURSES
FISH

This particular dish is best eaten hot, with plenty of Salt & Vinegar. The news print is a special delicacy and also provides something to read between the chips. These need not be over fried and should look slightly pasty. An over burnt chip could be a fried fag end — which might indicate carelessness on the part of the Chef. Although very similar to a real chip the taste can often be unpleasant. Avoid buying here again, I have found the 'News of the World' the most tasty. An oily version of Diana Dors can do a lot for a sensitive palette. After eating, scrumple up and drop in someones front garden.

Ruskin Spear

R.A. 1954

Born: 1911. Studied: Hammersmith School Art; RCA under Sir William Rothenstein.
Pres. London Group 1949. Portraits include: Sir Lawrence Olivier as Macbeth;
Dr Ramsey, Archbishop of Canterbury; Harold Wilson; 5th Duke of Westminster.
Works exhibited: Moscow, Paris, USA, Belgium, S Africa,
Australia, New Zealand. C.B.E. 1979

One thing I can't stand is eating alone. I have to have someone there, if not my wife, then someone else, doesn't matter how awful they are, but I have to have someone.

I can't entertain at home very easily as I live in the studio. I couldn't bear the idea of going round picking up the fag ends afterwards!

I think the shape of food is important. A Scotch Egg should look like a Scotch Egg – not like a Henry Moore.

I always have a banana for breakfast – if I feel up to it. I tell you what I do like, those fried bits you put in soup – croutons. My mother used to make a bacon roll and bread and butter pudding, lovely stuff. If you saw it in a pull-up for lorries you never knew if it was flies or currants on top!

I can't stand tripe or those things people have with custard when their insides don't work – prunes. I HATE them! Do you know why? I went to a school for crippled children and we were always given prunes. We used to flip the stones at each other when we'd finished. There was a horrible nurse who disliked me and she used to make me crawl about under the tables picking them up.

A special meal? I'll have smoked herring, Roast Beef and Yorkshire and one of those things in little plastic buckets – yoghurt!

Anthony Green

R.A. 1977

Born: 1939. Studied: Slade School. Member London Group. Won various art prizes.
Works in: Tate; Brazil; USA; Wales; Belfast; Tokyo.

I was thoroughly spoilt as a small boy because my Grandfather was Chef to the Waldorf from 1917 to 1940. Every Sunday we used to eat with my grandparents and we used to have amazing four course meals all cooked by my Grandfather. He maintained that the quality of food was killed by the First World War and that nowadays nobody has ever eaten really good food.

A silly thing that drives me mad – I like eclairs but in England they are always filled with fresh cream – they should have crème patissiere.

I think most creative people are interested in cooking. They are creative on all levels not just painting.

One of the great inventions that England has given to the world is Marmite. I have it every morning for breakfast and two pieces of toast.

When we entertain we have a dinner and give them the works. All the wedding presents get dragged out. It's usually a three course meal, probably smoked salmon, a roast and for dessert it would be a monstrous creation of cream, meringue and strawberries that looks a bit like the Taj Mahal!

We have a green enamel gas cooker that my mother bought in 1947. It hasn't any high technological details but we've still got it. In fact, the family joke is that "when Dad's boat comes in we'll have a new cooker!"

Homard Newbourg

2 lbs cooked lobster meat	
3 oz butter	
1 tblsp oil	
Lobster coral if possible	
Brandy (mini bottle!)	
1 carton of double cream	
Pepper and salt (subtly)	

Cut lobster into pieces, toss in melted butter and one tablespoon of oil until hot (oil is to prevent butter turning brown) – pause – add coral – toss gently/ season.

Pour brandy over lobster, mixing gently but well, finally stir in the cream. Keep hot. Serve with Riz Creole. NB. The coral adds a blush to the sauce.

Elisabeth Frink

R.A. 1977

I read quite a lot of cookery books and I do follow several recipes in a general way. If I am doing a complicated recipe for the first time I probably do it correctly and thereafter use the recipe in a very free way. I don't very often bother about precise measurements except, of course, when making things like pastry.

I think cooking is a very creative pastime and most of my artist friends are very good cooks. I think you have to enjoy food to be interested in it and to cook it well.

Recently we have been eating far less meat, as I think a lot of meat is full of impurities. I avoid eating chicken, veal and pork because most of these meats that you buy in the shops are battery reared. I believe that even the beef in this country is injected with hormones. Lamb is the most naturally reared meat that we still have. We like eating fish a great deal but it is sometimes difficult to get interesting fish in the country. We are fortunate, however, in that our local fishmonger will get us things if we order them, such as mussels. Apart from that we do eat a lot of vegetables which we grow ourselves.

I do mind very much about eating natural foods and we are very lucky to have a good wholefood shop near us. Many people have not got access to these shops which are few and far between and in many cases cannot afford to buy their products.

I like to cook for an occasion and we entertain a great deal.

Prawn and Yoghurt Quiche

Shortcrust pastry
5 ozs butter or margarine
1 small egg
12 ozs plain flour
Water
Filling
1 small onion
½ lb packet frozen prawns
1 tblsp sunflower oil
6 eggs
1 large 15 oz container yoghurt
1 cup of milk
Pepper and salt

I use a lot of yoghurt in cooking and always in quiches instead of cream.

Make pastry and line 10 inch flan dish. Sauté onion chopped fine and defrosted prawns briefly in sunflower oil – do not overcook.

Beat up eggs, yoghurt and milk and add seasoning.

I cook the pastry and the filling at the same time so spread the prawns and onions evenly over the pastry case and tip in the mixture of eggs and yoghurt.

Cook for 30-40 minutes in a pre-heated oven at 350°/Reg 4. This recipe can be used very well with mushrooms instead of prawns.

Ivor Roberts-Jones

R.A. 1973

Born: 1913. Studied: Goldsmith's College; RA Schools. Sculptor. Public commissions: Winston Churchill, Parliament Square; Augustus John Memorial, Fordingbridge. Portraits include: Somerset Maugham, Yehudi Menuhin, The Duke of Edinburgh, Paul Claudel. Publications on sculpture and poetry. C.B.E. 1975.

Yes, food should certainly be a pleasure, and not just fuel, but then so should cookery books. They are only too often just fuel and no great pleasure to read. Alice B. Toklas describes her cooking in vivid terms. About wild duck she says that the oven should have two doors, be brought up to the highest possible temperature, and the duck persuaded to fly in at one door and out at the other, when it will be nicely done. This is "Nouvelle Cuisine," with its rapid cooking in the oven, well before its time.

I do cook from time to time. I don't so much remember successful recipes as times when things turned out especially well. With all the care in the world there are variations and high moments – little miracles even – and awful boobs. I find I always seem to need help at "serving up" time.

My studio is just across the garden from the kitchen. The advantages are all mine. My wife complains that her knives, bowls and sieves are always walking across. When I'm casting, buckets are in short supply, and brushes and dust pans and even shovels all walk from time to time.

Talking of food and drink – smoked eels and Schnaps, served at an Academy dinner, struck me as an ideal combination. Smoked eels, trout smoked mildly, and smoked chicken, are all part of the Suffolk scene which we enjoy.

I would find it difficult to settle on a favourite meal, but I would pay serious attention to any mention of lobster, Charollais beef, and for dessert, a Doyenne du Comice. But, of course, a well grown James Grieve apple and a piece of cheese on a sunny day in the garden is perfect too.

Sculptors and food as a subject brings up two snippets. Rodin preferred English food to French – the plainer the better. And Bernini, late in life anyway, ate very sparsely and mainly fruit.

Salmon or Hake en Papillote

The quantities are for four people

3½ oz carrots

3½ onions, peeled

1½ oz butter

3½ oz button mushrooms

1 level tsp of freshly chopped tarragon

4 tblsp of olive oil

1½ lbs approx. of salmon or hake

12 tarragon leaves

3 oz softened butter

8 tblsp dry white wine

5 tblsp of chicken stock

2 finely chopped shallots

Salt and freshly ground pepper

4 sheets of greaseproof paper or aluminium foil

This recipe is for salmon as a treat or for hake when everyday.

Put the sliced carrots and onions into the butter to soften. Add the mushrooms after five minutes and cook for a further three minutes. Stir to prevent sticking. Add the tarragon and season, cover and cook for a further two minutes. Allow to cool.

Brush the foil with the oil. Pre-heat the oven to 480°F (Mark 9). Fold the foil into papillotes keeping the oil inside and put ¼ of the vegetables into each. Carve the salmon, or hake (the hake may have to be cut diagonally) into slices about ½ in. thick. Place three slices into each papillote on top of the Julienne and add to each three tarragon leaves, ¾ oz of butter in small pieces, two tablespoons of white wine and one of stock. Turn up and seal the

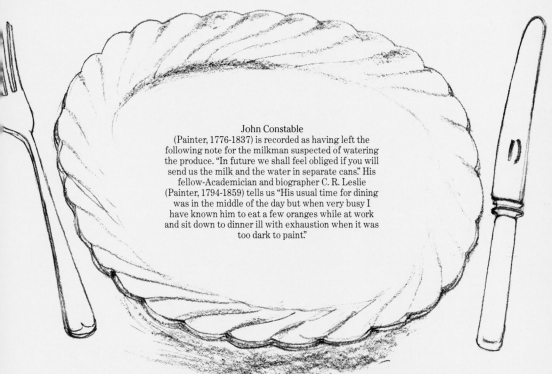

John Constable
(Painter, 1776-1837) is recorded as having left the
following note for the milkman suspected of watering
the produce. "In future we shall feel obliged if you will
send us the milk and the water in separate cans." His
fellow-Academician and biographer C. R. Leslie
(Painter, 1794-1859) tells us "His usual time for dining
was in the middle of the day but when very busy I
have known him to eat a few oranges while at work
and sit down to dinner ill with exhaustion when it was
too dark to paint."

papillotes after seasoning the contents with chopped shallot, salt and pepper.

Brush a roasting dish with oil and heat the dish in the oven for five minutes. Place the papillotes in the dish and do *not* allow them to touch. Place in the oven and cook for 4-6 minutes. Domestic ovens may well not heat up as efficiently as those in restaurants, so six minutes may be advisable the first time. Serve them as they are.

A Beurre Blanc should be served separately, so that each guest can add his own after opening up his papillote.

Beurre Blanc

3 oz of butter cut into little cubes
3 tblsp of white wine vinegar
5 tblsp of dry white wine
1 tsp finely chopped shallot
1 tblsp double cream
Salt and pepper

Put the white wine vinegar, white wine and shallots into a small saucepan and reduce until you are left with about 2 tablespoons of liquid. Add the cream and as it comes to the boil turn the heat down very, very low and gradually add the cubes of butter, whisking continuously with a wire whisk. Keep whisking until all the butter is incorporated, add salt and pepper, strain through a fine wire sieve hot.

N.B. If you have to make this sauce in advance it can be reheated, very gently whisking continuously, but it is better to serve it as soon as it is made. *(C.C)*

Roger de Grey

R.A. 1969

Born: 1918. Studied: Chelsea School Art. Lecturer and Master of Painting,
Kings College, Newcastle-upon-Tyne; Senior Tutor, RCA; Principal City and Guilds
London. Works in: Great Britain and Australia.

I not only cook but I grow the food I cook as well. Ever since I was a small boy I've liked hors d'oeuvres better than anything else. But the recipe I'll give you is for trout. I love all food but I'm becoming more and more a vegetarian cook. I've just come back from Hong Kong and I do like Chinese cookery. We had the most delicious Chinese food, all the vegetables cooked very quickly in a "Wok." They grow very good vegetables there.

I think cooking is creative and most artists do it well. They probably had to in their student days, in a pan on a gas ring, and that started them off. My favourite lunch is raw Brussels sprouts salad. I make a very good smoked mackerel pâté, to go with it.

Years ago we used to entertain a lot and take people out to French and Italian restaurants, now we really can't afford it and anyway the food is not as good as if we had cooked it at home. I suppose my favourite meal would be the kind of thing you used to get in the South of France before the war, when the waiter came with dishes piled high with all kinds of hors d'oeuvres, things that you've never eaten before. That would really be enough but if I had to follow it, I'd have something like escalopes de veau. I love wine, but I'm not a wine snob, I can drink wines that other people call disgusting, though of course I like really good wines – although not at £25 a bottle.

Poached Trout

Chopped onion	
Trout	
Salt and pepper	
White wine	
Fennel	
Parsley	

Fry onion till soft, put in a dish and put the trout on top, season it with salt and pepper and cover with white wine. Add herbs and bake.

Craigie Aitchison

A.R.A. 1978

Born: 1926. Studied: Slade School. Received British Council and Italian Government Scholarship for Painting. Exhibited: England; Tokyo; Bologna and Paris. Works in Tate; CAS; Scottish Nationᵃl Gallery of Modern Art; NG Melbourne, Australia.

The things I like are Egg Mayonnaise (homemade) with lamb chops or fishfingers. I also like scrambled eggs made without milk, with sausages, bacon, tomatoes and mushrooms, lemon sole (filleted) and mackerel; leek soup and consommé (the one in a tin).

Herrings in Oatmeal

2 good herrings

Handful of pin head oatmeal (fine ground)

Salt and freshly ground pepper

Butter

Herrings are very good fried in pin-head oatmeal and butter.

Mix the oatmeal with the salt and pepper on a board or plate and pat onto the opened filleted fish. Fry in butter, top first, so that they end skin side down. They take about 2½ minutes on each side depending on the size of the fish.

Batter for Fish
An old recipe from Ceres, Fife.

6 oz flour

½ tsp salt

½ tsp baking soda

1 tsp cream of tartar

1 egg

Water to mix

Mix all ingredients together well – the consistency should be fairly thick and creamy. Dip small pieces of fish in batter then deep fry in very hot cooking oil until crisp and golden and puffed up. Drain well and serve hot with lemon.

Elizabeth Blackadder R.A.

Colin Hayes

R.A. 1970

Born 1919. Studied: Ruskin School Drawing. Senior Tutor RCA.
Work in: Arts Council; British Council; Carlisle Museum.
Publications: Renoir; Stanley Spencer; Rembrandt; articles in journals on art.

Dishes cooked with sorrel feature as expensive delicacies only because it is difficult to buy. But it is easy to grow and well worth planting, as it takes care of itself year after year and makes a fine flavouring.

Sorrel suits almost any fish which can be baked.

Fish Baked with Sorrel

Butter
Cut or fillet of fish
Sorrel
Pepper and salt
½ glass dry white wine

Butter a sheet of baking foil. (Cut foil large enough to make a bag, not a tight fitting parcel.) Wrap the fish in enough leaves of sorrel to cover it. Place on the foil and make an open bag. Season with salt and pepper and pour in wine. Seal the bag so as to contain the juices and place in a low-medium oven for about 20 minutes. Serve with the juices.

This is a very simple recipe but remember Escoffier's "faites simple," and do not spoil the sorrel flavour by elaborating with herbs.

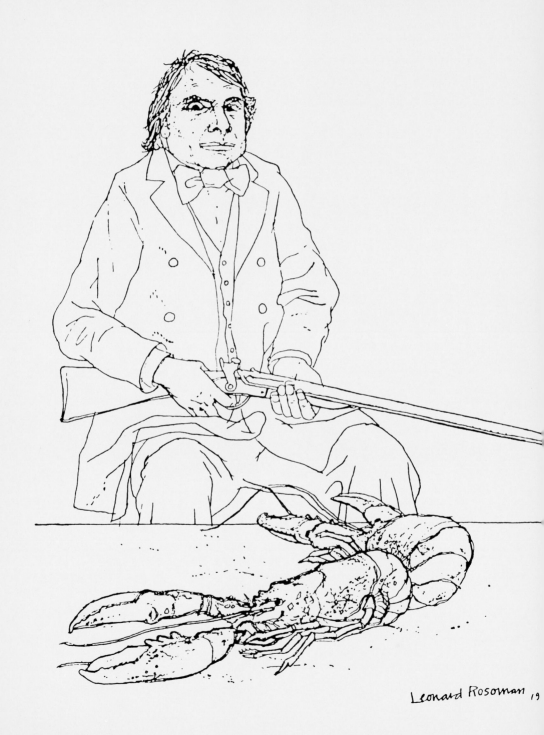

Leonard Rosoman 19

Leonard Rosoman

R.A. 1969

Born: 1913. Studied: King Edward VII School Art, Durham Univ.; Central School;
RA School. Official War Artist. Executed mural paintings: Festival Britain, 1951; British
Pavilion, Brussels World Fair, 1958; Harewood House. Taught in many art schools. O.B.E. 1981

This sounds awfully boring but my food is geared to my work and to a very flexible low fat diet. What I eat in the middle of the day is absolutely to do with the fact that I have to go on working afterwards, so dinner is always the most important meal. It's extraordinary that when you look at the whole culinary scene all the very good rich food is bad for you.

I do have an enormously varied diet, I never feel deprived. A cold plate at lunch and a two course meal at dinner is delicious. On the protein level I tend to avoid the rich things, steak and lamb. I eat a lot of fish, I get satisfaction from enjoying something that is good for me. I'm very fond of wine but drink no spirits at all. At the end of the day, I should find it very difficult to give up my aperitif. I should feel very deprived without it.

The dining room in our house is a very important room. When we moved in, it was the only room we didn't like; it was a sort of underground bunker. I've now painted the whole room with an elaborate mural and had a very special and beautiful marble table put in, so the evening meal is a kind of occasion. We eat breakfast and lunch in another small room, it's cosy and gets the sun in the morning and is very pleasant. Breakfast, by the way, is a thing that I get. I'm a very good early riser – I think painters are because of catching the morning light.

A favourite meal? Perhaps potted shrimps, and escalopes of veal done in sage butter. I think my favourite kind of food is very good, well cooked, nursery food! My wife says I eat more potatoes than anyone she's ever known. I cook small new potatoes for lunch with salad, and even eat cold potatoes with an aperitif! My wife has literally hundreds of cook books and I've illustrated some, so, yes, we do look at cookbooks.

Steamed Lobsters Amagansett

2 Lobsters of 1½ to 2 lbs
Beer
Butter
Lemons

Take two live lobsters each weighing 1½ to 2 lbs. Store in the fridge until time for cooking but be sure to cook them the same day they are bought.

Use a deep pot large enough to take the lobsters easily on the bottom. Fill the pot with 2 inches of beer and bring to the boil. Plunge the lobsters in head first. Cover, return to the boil, then reduce heat and simmer for 5 minutes for the first pound and 3 minutes for each additional pound.

Remove the lobsters from the pot, place on their backs and using a heavy sharp-pointed knife split them from end to end starting at the head. Retain the green liver (tomalley) and (in female lobsters) the roe (coral). Remove the sand sack from the head and the intestinal track which runs down the tail section near the back.

Serve with clarified butter and lemon wedges.

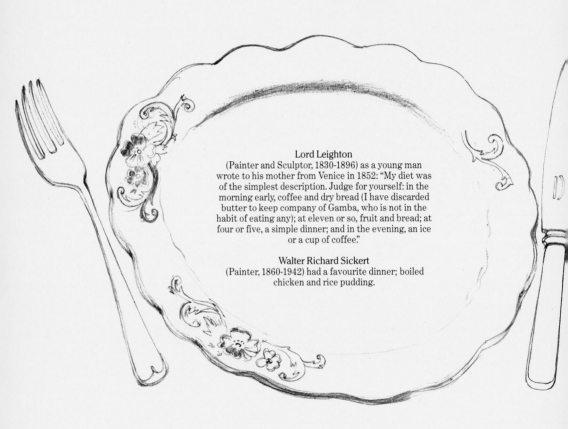

Lord Leighton
(Painter and Sculptor, 1830-1896) as a young man
wrote to his mother from Venice in 1852: "My diet was
of the simplest description. Judge for yourself: in the
morning early, coffee and dry bread (I have discarded
butter to keep company of Gamba, who is not in the
habit of eating any); at eleven or so, fruit and bread; at
four or five, a simple dinner; and in the evening, an ice
or a cup of coffee."

Walter Richard Sickert
(Painter, 1860-1942) had a favourite dinner; boiled
chicken and rice pudding.

Betty Swanwick

R.A. 1979

Born: 1915. Studied: Goldsmith's College School of Art; R.C.A. Three books written
and illustrated. Posters for L.P.T.B., murals for various organisations. Water colourist.

I don't like: Eels, skate, venison, jugged hare, duck, tripe and I wouldn't touch veal – they are kept so wretchedly. I'm more than half vegetarian, I dislike red meat.

I entertain at home but often if visitors come down from London they take me out because they know I am not partial to cooking. I do simple cooking but am not at all keen on it. There are a number of quite good little restaurants around that are reasonable and are a great help. A favourite meal?

Well, it would be fish and asparagus. I love that. I like terribly ordinary food, bread and honey, apples and baked custards, all rather English things. I take orange juice last thing at night. I'm rather keen on vitamin tablets.

Fish Pie

1 lb of cod

2 bay leaves

Salt and pepper

2 tsp of lemon juice

¼ lb mushrooms

1½ oz butter

1½ oz cornflour

Chopped parsley

1 tblsp of mayonnaise

1 pint of prawns

Approx. 1 lb of creamed potatoes

Cover cod and bay leaves with water. Add salt, pepper and two teaspoons of lemon juice. Poach for 10 minutes. Strain off juice from fish. Skin the fish (save the skin for cats). Place fish in buttered bakedish. Lightly fry mushrooms in a little butter and place on tissue paper. Put 1 oz of butter in a saucepan, add cornflour, stir in slowly the fish juice, adding the parsley and mayonnaise when the sauce has thickened. Peel prawns and put in cod and then add the mushrooms. Pour sauce on to fish and mix gently. Cover over with creamed potatoes. Dot the top with knobs of butter. Place in middle shelf of a moderately warmed oven and cook until crisp and brown – about twenty five or thirty minutes.

Norman Adams

R.A. 1972

Born: 1927. Studied: Harrow Art School and RCA. Head of School of painting
Manchester College of Art and Design. Exhibited: most European capitals and USA.
Paintings in collections of Tate and most
British Provincial galleries.
Works include decoration for ballets;
Covent Garden and Sadlers Wells.

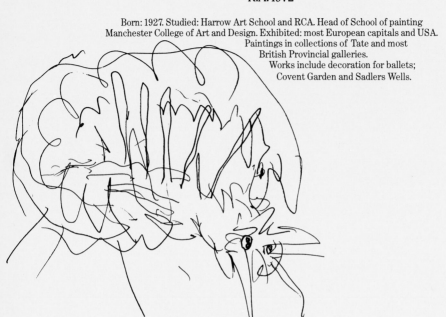

Lobster à La Scarp
(Scarp is an Uttermost Outer Hebride).

Scarp is an uninhabited island – where the pantry contains very little but fish and often resembles a fishmonger's slab. Fish eating becomes a duty – but lobster eating is never a duty. First catch your crustacean, or is it an arthropod? Wrestle with your conscience and drop it face first into boiling sea water having first stunned it by putting it under cold tap of fresh water. Twenty minutes turns it red and thoroughly dead, then dissect it – removing long thin black gut. Crack claws etc. – break into reasonable sized chunks so that it can be fairly distributed between ravenous fishermen.

Make a sauce with various substitutes for the proper ingredients – ie margarine, wholemeal flour, fake milk – there is a shortage of everything on Scarp. Chop up an onion and sizzle – mix sauce, onion and lobster chunks together – sprinkle with chopped mint which grows plentifully in abandoned gardens – serve about midnight, by oil lamp light. The more lobsters (and ditto fishermen) the better – to be followed by a ghastly oversweet pudding made by boiling tins of condensed milk for 2 or 3 hours so that the contents congeal to a kind of tooth-rotting fudge. Then tea drinking by driftwood fire.

Fish Quenelles

Fish

2 lb cleaned fresh fish (salmon, sole or a lean close-grained fish)

1 tblsp salt

Mixture

1 tblsp cornflour

¼ tsp finely pounded mace

1 litre cold boiled milk

¼ lb butter

1 egg

Preparation Remove all skin, bones and sinew from the fish and mince the fish four times. Sprinkle with salt and mince another four times. Cool in refrigerator and mince twice more (10 times in all). Use the trimmings to make a fish-bouillon (see 'cooking').

Place the cold minced raw fish, cornflour, mace and butter in the electric mixer and stir well with the pastry blender attachment. Add the cold boiled milk a spoonful at a time taking care that no fish remains unblended on the mixer attachment, blend it well till a soft mixture results. Then add the whole egg and blend gently.

Cooking Prepare a litre of bouillon from the cooked fish skin and bones, onion, bayleaf, peppercorn, lemon juice and white wine. Strain it into a saucepan and allow it to simmer.

Shape the prepared fish into ovals with dessertspoons dipped in iced water, and lower them gently into the slowly simmering bouillon. It is important that they boil slowly otherwise they disintegrate. Cook for about 3 minutes on one side, turn them over with a slotted spoon and cook for another 3-4 minutes on the other side till they are ready. Then remove them from the bouillon with the slotted spoon and place them on a large flat dish to cool.

Sauce To prepare the sauce blend a tablespoon flour and an equal amount of butter in a separate saucepan and add sufficient bouillon in which the quenelles were cooked. Add tarragon, mushroom cream etc. to flavour.

Serving Put quenelles in a buttered gratin dish, heat through thoroughly and pour on the sauce.

Maureen Harris
SECRETARY, FRIENDS

Fish Mayonnaise

serves 6.

1½ lbs halibut or turbot

Good bunch of parsley

10 peppercorns

1 onion halved

1 teaspoon salt

1 lb peeled prawns (fresh)

2 medium sized onions – finely chopped

Juice of 2 lemons

6 fl ozs olive oil (or enough to cover fish)

Freshly ground black pepper

½ pint of mayonnaise *(recipe below)*

1 clove garlic – optional but preferable

for decoration

Lettuce or watercress, black olives, parsley, a few prawns

Place fish (turbot or halibut), parsley stalks, peppercorns, onion and salt in a saucepan with enough water to cover. Bring to boil and simmer gently for 10 mins or until just cooked. Leave in water to cool.

Take out – remove skin and bones and divide into chunks (mouthful size).

In a bowl place the cooked fish, prawns, finely chopped onions, chopped parsley, juice of lemons and the olive oil. Season with salt and ground pepper.

Marinate for at least 2 hours preferably overnight in the refrigerator.

Also prepare mayonnaise the day before. Store in the refrigerator.

2 egg yolks

¼ pint olive oil

1 tblsp lemon juice

½ tsp caster sugar

½ tsp dry mustard

Salt and pepper to taste

1 clove of garlic crushed

Place all ingredients into liquidiser (except oil), mix lightly and add oil very slowly – until desired consistency is reached.

To serve Drain the fish. Place in a serving dish on or surrounded by lettuce or watercress. Cover with the mayonnaise and garnish with a few shelled prawns, olives and parsley. Return to refrigerator and then eat within 1 hour.

This makes a very good main course served with new potatoes and a salad – or on its own as a starter.

Dr Gerald Libby
PROFESSOR OF ANATOMY

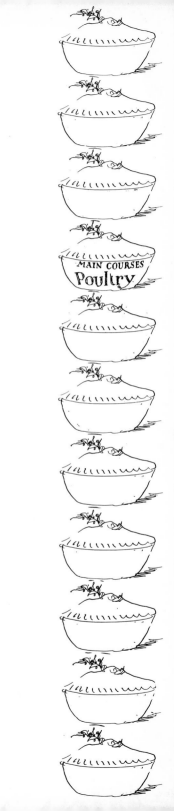

MAIN COURSES
Poultry

RSPCA + Sir Peter Scott

JR Bratby

John Bratby

R.A. 1971

Born: 1928. Painter and writer; Member of London Group. Studied: Kingston School Art; RCA. Taught at: Carlisle College Art; RCA. Gained various prizes and scholarships and exhibited in numerous galleries in Britain and abroad. Appeared on TV and radio. Contributed illustrations for Oxford Illustrated Old Testament, 1968.

I obtained the recipe for Monastery Honeyed Duck specially for this book. The Restaurant is hung with my paintings and drawings and when I can afford it, I go and have their honey roasted duck with Guinness to drink, after drawing in the country. I always have the duck totally boned. Bird seems to be my favourite meat. Apart from that, the food I most enjoy is a bacon, eggs, mushrooms, toast and tomato breakfast cooked by my wife Patti.

I dislike garlic greatly (but cannot taste it in the honeyed duck). Rice pudding and tapioca pudding I loathe too. I was given it every day, aged 5, in hospital. Also mayonnaise, vinegar, steak tartare and onions – unless fried, then I adore them. I'm not too fond of spaghetti, though its bearable with a rich, heavy Italian dressing eaten in Italy with rough wine.

When I was at the Royal College of Art, I cooked breakfast in a pan in the Mural School on a Valor Oil stove. I painted a picture of an egg in a pan on the stove on hardboard 20″ x 30″ and put it in the R.A. Summer Show, collecting it later as rejected. In dejection and enjoying the theatrical gesture, I threw the masterpiece over the fence on to a building site!

My student love was baked beans fried slowly in butter and put on buttered toast. I remembered this with such delight that I wrote about it in one of my novels and it so impressed one of the critics that he said in his review that he'd try it! But never since has the dish tasted as it did when in rags I'd call on the now head of York Art School, who would look at me with disgust, and then add another seal on his passport to Heaven, usher me up the Victorian stairs, and make me baked beans as only he could do.

Monastery recipe for Honey Roasted Duck

4½ lb duckling – for 2 people
Rosemary
Red wine
Orange zest and juice
2 onions sliced and fried
Honey
Garlic
Black pepper and salt
1 tsp cornflour
1 sliced orange, watercress and chopped parsley

Prick ducklings all over with sharp fork. Cover ducklings with slightly salted water, add generous rosemary, and simmer for 45 minutes.

Drain ducks and put in roasting tin without fat or oil and cook for 1 hour at 350°F.

Meanwhile reduce stock by ⅔ and remove duck fat (keep, very good for cooking). Add the same quantity of red wine and reduce again by half allowing or leaving to simmer, with lots of orange zest and fried onions.

Remove ducks from oven and coat with honey which has been melted and had crushed garlic added to taste (and black pepper). Return to hot oven 400°F/Reg. 6 and cook until brown, about 20 minutes.

Make sauce with pan juices, fat removed, and wine – stock reduction. Thicken with a little cornflour mixed with orange juice. The duck can have the meat removed in two halves from the breast-bone and spine leaving only wings and legbones in.

Put on plate, pour sauce over and decorate with slices of orange, watercress and chopped parsley.

Edward Wolfe

R.A. 1972

Born: 1897. Studied: Slade School, under Tonks and Wilson Steer; Omega Workshop;
Paris; Florence; won scholarships at Regent St. Polytechnic School of Art. Designed
costume and stage set for Cochran's Revue, 1931 and 'Stream Line', 1933.
Exhibited in numerous galleries. Worked with BBC.

Food is a *great* pleasure to me. I've had great fun in my life because wherever I've been, in the world, I've learnt to cook a meal from the people I've been with. I do still cook occasionally. I'm a reasonable cook, I've even made some of my own inventions. I'm very very interested in food. I like Mexican food, it's lovely, some is very hot and spicy, some isn't. Moroccan food is very good, too. I must give you some dishes.

O yes, I certainly think there is a connection between painting and cooking, it's a very creative thing. Breakfast? Sometimes I have scrambled or boiled eggs, sometime I just have a bit of cake and sometimes I don't feel like food at all. If I have a big lunch I have a very little supper, just a sandwich or something.

We entertain at home mostly and one is sometimes a bit pretentious and tries to make something amusing. What would I give? Hors d'oeuvres or melon, some little fish nonsense, then perhaps I'd have a duck. I do a boned duck for parties. I stuff it with everything except the kitchen stove and my girl friends! I often do it with various fruits and serve it cold. We usually give parties in the studio and make them as fantastic as possible. I'm rather keen on puddings, fruity ones and strange sweet dishes. I am very fond of wines though at the moment I'm not supposed to have any. I do have some cookbooks because I like all kinds of cookery.

Mole Verde

1 turkey	
3 onions	
Salt	
2 lb green tomatoes (hard)	
2 cloves garlic	
½ lb lard or oil	
¼ lb walnuts	
¼ lb almonds unblanched	
12 chillies or 7 green peppers	
½ lb pumpkin seeds	

This recipe will serve 12.

Cut turkey into pieces and boil in water with an onion and salt. Fry pumpkin seeds and unblanched almonds, walnuts and chillies. Peel and mash tomatoes with another onion and the garlic and fry in some of the lard. Add the nuts, chillies, pumpkin seeds and two pints of the turkey stock with the boiled turkey. Season with salt and simmer till thickens.

N.B. Mexican green tomatoes are not the same as our unripe green tomatoes but are cousins to the Cape Gooseberry. They can be bought in tins, or you can use ordinary unripe tomatoes *(C.C.)*

Kyffin Williams

R.A. 1974

Born: 1918. Studied: Slade School. Senior Art Master Highgate School 1944-73.
Hon. M.A. University of Wales. Exhibited in several galleries.
Publication: Across the Straits (autobiography) 1973.

As I am without exception the worst cook west of the Iron Curtain, it is entirely appropriate that I should contribute the secrets of my poisonous culinary efforts to the book for circulation by members of the CIA at certain specialised personal targets East of the curtain. It might solve not only the problems of the R.A. but also of the world as well.

I could dispense my vast knowledge but that might, of course, turn the Friends into enemies.

Pastai Brain Bach (Rook Pie)

Rooks

Short pastry

Chives

Thyme

Stock

Bacon, chopped

Only the meat from the breasts of young rooks is used and put in a pie dish lined with short pastry. Chopped bacon, chives, and thyme are added, the meat seasoned and a little stock added. The pie is then covered with pastry and baked in a moderate oven.

Allan Gwynne-Jones

R.A. 1965

Born: 1892. Studied: Slade School. Professor of Painting, R.C.A. till 1930. Staff of Slade
School. Trustee, Tate Gallery 1939-44. Work in collections of: HM The Queen;
HM The Queen Mother; Tate and other public galleries. Published works on art. C.B.E.1980

In 1911 I was still a law student living in rooms in Cheyne Walk costing 8 shillings a week. I had an allowance of £75 a year for four years, but chianti was 5d a bottle and dinner in Soho cost 1/6d and a seat at the Ballet 2/6d and I could walk there and back. If I sold a picture for £5 that was riches for a month.

Most of my friends were at the Slade. I well remember a wonderful afternoon in October when Randolph Schwabe came to the law courts and fetched me away to the Slade to see Stanley Spencer's "Nativity," which had just won the summer composition prize; Brown was Slade Professor and Steer and Tonks were on the staff.

The Royal Academy I am sorry to say, was regarded as a sinful place and few of my friends ever set foot in it and neither did I until twenty years later.

In 1935, before I was married I lived in Fitzroy St. I cooked for myself. When I enter-tained, my guests were usually given chicken casserole for supper.

Mrs. Ireland (who 'did for me' and was paid 7/6d a week) got

the vegetables ready for the pot. They were shallots, carrots, mushrooms and potatoes, I cut up the chicken with nail scissors. Mrs. Ireland sliced the potatoes and carrots to the size of thick 50ps.

I came home from teaching at the Slade at lunch time.

I ground black pepper and salt on to the chicken and vegetables and fried them separately in butter – just browning them, I also added sugar to the carrots. I put the chicken in the bottom of the casserole then the mushrooms (I didn't fry these), then the carrots, the shallots and the potatoes on top with a layer of Bay leaves and then I opened a tin or two of Turkish Vine Leaves stuffed with rice and packed them tight on top, put on the lid and returned to the Slade to teach until four o'clock. Then quick back to Fitzroy Street to put the casserole into a very slow oven ready for eight o'clock.

Wild strawberries or figs when possible for pudding and some cheese. I opened red wine.

No fridge in those days. I collected a block of ice in newspaper from the fishmonger, hammered it and put it into a bucket for the white wine. Then I think I laid the table, had a bath, listened to Monteverdi and waited until the doorbell rang.

Chicken Casserole

1 fresh chicken	1 lb mushrooms
1 lb shallots	Bay leaves, Seasoning
1 lb potatoes	1 large tin of stuffed Turkish Vine leaves
1 lb carrots	*Preparation* see above

Elizabeth Blackadder,

R.A. 1976

Born: 1931. Studied: Edinburgh College of Art where she now teaches. Member of
Royal Scottish Academy. Work represented in international public collections.

Food is a pleasure just as much visually for me as in any other sense. I like looking at markets with mounds of fruit and vegetables, at windows of bakers' shops with cakes and fruit tarts of all shapes and colours although I am seldom tempted to eat sweet things. I get a great deal of enjoyment from looking at still life painting of food. I enjoy the sheer skill of the painter who can depict the bloom on peaches and plums, the texture of oysters or the drops of juice from a peeled lemon. Nearly all the painters I know are seriously interested in food, in eating and in cooking.

Boiled Fowl, Oatmeal Pudding and Leek Soup

1 boiling fowl or not so young chicken

3-4 leeks, chopped

2 onions chopped

Handful rice

A few prunes (optional)

For oatmeal pudding

4 tblsp oatmeal

2 tblsp Atora or shredded suet

Salt and pepper

1 medium onion chopped

This is an easy old Scottish recipe – simple and economical and easy to prepare as you get 2 courses in one.

Take a large pot, fill with water place fowl in it and boil until fowl is tender – couple of hours or so depending on size and toughness. Keep skimming fat from boiling stock.

Mix the ingredients for the oatmeal pudding and moisten with hot stock – don't make it too wet. Dip clean cloth in hot stock, flour the cloth well and tie pudding lightly in cloth with string but allow room for expansion.

About ¾ hour before fowl is ready put pudding in pot with fowl and boil together. About ½ hour before fowl is ready throw in chopped leeks, onions, handful of rice and if you like, a few prunes. When ready lift out fowl and oatmeal pudding and keep hot while you serve the soup (which is the stock from the pot).

A mushroom sauce goes well with chicken and oatmeal pudding and helps keep it moist.

Paul Hogarth

A.R.A. 1974

Born: 1917. Studied: Manchester College Art; St Martin's. Illustrator and draughtsman.
Travelled extensively: France, Germany, Morocco, Russia, Spain, USA, China, S. Africa,
Poland. Fascination with American urban landscape – "America Observed"
(with Stephen Spender, 1979). Collaborated with Brendan Behan, Robert Graves,
Malcolm Muggeridge on other topographical works.

Needless-to say, I love good food, but who can afford to eat out regularly nowadays? Small and low-priced good restaurants are few and far between although they are more common in Spain where I spend half the year.

For some years I was a single parent looking after a son with an appetite like the proverbial horse. Restaurant meals were therefore out of the question. So I decided to put myself through a course of basic, gourmet cooking. I absorbed a lot of information from girlfriends and housewives, from restaurants and from cookbooks wherever we've lived, in Spain, in America and in Britain. Generally speaking, I've had to rely on what I could buy in the local supermarket. You *can* get good food and good wine at chainstores if you know just what to buy.

I look forward to an early breakfast – 7.30 am listening to music and enjoying real coffee, good wholemeal bread lightly toasted and a boiled Size A brown egg. I have a light lunch – just a sandwich or a salad with black coffee. In the evenings I go for casserole situations where you can put in your chosen meat, chops or beef, submerge them in soy sauce and surround them with peppers and mushrooms and herbs. I try to reduce the time spent in the kitchen by cooking all the elements of an agreeable meal in one dish. Then I try not to get involved in a lot of separate vegetables, supplementing a main dish with a mixed freshly-made salad. Fruit and cheese to follow, not a lot of high calorie desserts.

Cooking is creative, it's a therapy, like painting. And it is especially so if you are cooking just for yourself. If you work alone as artists do, you need to have these breaks in working time where you take pleasure in physical activity and prepare food carefully.

Chicken C'an Bi

Sufficient for 4-6 people

1 fresh whole roasting chicken cut into 8 pieces

1 x 5 fl oz bottle Soy sauce

2 large onions

2 red peppers

¼ lb fresh mushrooms

2 tblsp cooking oil

½ clove garlic or granules

Rosemary

Black pepper

Marinade chicken pieces in bowl of soy sauce. Cover and leave in fridge for at least one hour. Meanwhile, slice the onions, the two red peppers and detach stalks from mushrooms.

Pour the cooking oil into a large open earthenware casserole (but if unavailable, roasting tin will suffice).

Make a bed of the onions and peppers, placing the chicken portions on top. Sprinkle/squeeze the garlic granules or juice on to the portions adding the rosemary and black pepper. Arrange the rest of peppers and mushrooms around the chicken portions. Roast for 1½ hours at Gas 4, 350°F.

Serve with light dry red wine – a good Rioja e.g. Rioja Berberana, Cata de Plata or Grants of St James's Rioja (both obtainable from Victoria Wine).

Bernard Dunstan

R.A. 1968

Born: 1920. Studied: Byam Shaw School; Slade School. Member NEAC. President, Royal West of England Academy. Has published several books on painting. Pictures in many private collections, and NPG; Nat. Gall. of NZ; Bristol Art Gall.; London Museum; Arts Council.

I can cook a little: my soups and cakes are quite good, but there's not much I can do in between. I do a good birthday cake, with icing and decorations, rich and black: and the fruit doesn't all sink to the bottom. Diana does all the real cooking, though, and I take over when she's teaching – just a soup and something quite simple, but I quite enjoy doing it.

Cooking as a craft certainly has a connection with painting. For instance, I make up my own egg-and-oil emulsion primer, and that's very like mayonnaise. Both painting and cooking are sensual pleasures, or should be. I've never done any actual pictures of food, but I've often thought about a still-life of cakes and buns. Didn't Bonnard once do some petit fours? And Ruskin said he wanted to *eat up* all the palaces in Venice, stone by stone, by drawing them.

We don't do much entertaining. We're both painting, and Diana can't be expected to spend half the day cooking because someone is coming. So we eat out quite a lot.

I am very fond of Italian food, and we both thrive on it when we're in Italy; the plainness, and eating almost the same meal every day, seems to agree with us. And, of course, most important of all: lots of wine!

Chicken in Elder Flower Champagne

Elder Flower Champagne	1 small green pepper
12 panacles (heads) of elder flower	Plain flour – 1 tblsp
1 lemon sliced finely	Salt and pepper to taste
1½ lbs granulated sugar	½ pint elderflower champagne
2 tblsp white wine vinegar	½ lb mushrooms
1 gallon of water	
Chicken	
1 whole chicken	
Sunflower oil – approx half a cupful	
2 onions	
2 leeks (when in season)	
4 small turnips	

First make your champagne.

Collect, on a sunny morning, the elder flowers, and steep them in the water to which you have added the rest of the ingredients.

Do not use a metal container. Stir occasionally, cover, and leave for 24-36 hours. Strain through fine muslin (or nylon

stocking) into beer bottles. Screw down
firmly, displacing the liquid in each bottle
with the stopper. After about a week, test
for fermentation. When this has begun
ease stoppers one turn. Screw down firmly
again about three weeks later. Leave for
six weeks, after which time the champagne
is ready to drink or cook with.

In a fire proof casserole gently fry
the whole bird in the sunflower oil, turning
it at intervals, until at least the breasts are
golden brown. Remove onto a warm plate.
Sweat the sliced up onions in the oil until
transparent, add a tablespoon of water if
there is any likelihood of the onions

catching. Cut up the rest of the vegetables
and add to the onions. Stir them about for
a few moments.

Sprinkle with the flour to
which you have added the salt and pepper,
and stir about until the flour can be said to
have cooked for 3 mins. Pour on ½ pint
elder flower champagne or use from any
bottle that has failed to effervesce. Stir
about until the liquid has amalgamated
with the flour to make a thin sauce. Add
more water or stock if necessary. Add
mushrooms and chicken. Baste
over the chicken and cook for about 1 hour
at No. 2½ (gas), 310°F.

James Butler

R.A. 1972

Born 1931. Studied: Maidstone College Art; St Martin's; City and Guilds of London
Art School; RCA. Tutor, Sculpture and Drawing, City and Guilds School. National
Diploma Sculpture 1950. Major commissions:
Portrait statue Pres. Kenyatta; Monument to Freedom Fighters of Zambia.

I suppose that my tastes in food are most unexciting and rather simple. I am a cheese and onion man. I am very fond of cheese – very strong mature cheddar, gorgonzola, stilton, etc. My usual evening meal is a piece of cheese, an onion and a few potato crisps.

I am not very educated in wines, and much prefer a stiff whisky, water and lots of ice.

My wife, who could hardly boil an egg when we were first married is now an excellent cook – in fact when we were first married I used to cook the Sunday lunch, which is always the traditional roast.

She makes really nice spaghetti sauces and one of my favourite recipes is for her marinaded chicken pieces.

With reference to the R.A. – I remember that when I was elected an Associate – it is the usual custom for each new Member to make a brief speech on the first Varnishing Day Lunch that they attend – my speech was this:

Gentlemen, there are two reasons why I am pleased to be here today, one is that it is good to be a member of an organisation that is run by and for artists and the second is that I have never eaten so well in my life. (The Members' Varnishing Day Lunch must be the best cold meal in London).

Marinaded Chicken Pieces

Marinade
1 small onion, chopped
1 clove garlic, crushed
1 tblsp chopped parsley
Juice of lemon
1 tblsp sugar
1 tsp dried tarragon
2 cups white wine
Freshly ground pepper and a tsp of salt
½ cup wine vinegar

Mix all the ingredients together to make the marinade.

Leave 6 pieces of chicken in marinade for at least 6 hours – turning occasionally.

Roast in butter or olive oil (in pre-heated oven) gas mark 6 or 400F.

Or even better barbecue the pieces on a charcoal fire.

Vivian Pitchforth

R.A. 1953

Born: 1895. Studied: Wakefield School Art; Leeds School Art; RCA. Member London Group. Exhibited in various countries and works in collections in Britain and abroad.

I'm no Mrs. Beaton and not particularly a food enthusiast either. I only wish I could be. I get quite jealous when I see people happily stowing away large helpings of rich food: fried things, food tarted up and spiced, onions and pickles, all things I have to do without. So, this can only mean a "Weak tummy" and small helpings. This cuts out mostly feeding out in restaurants. The helpings are too large and the Yorkshireman in me hates leaving more than half of it.

However, leaving out the pig, except its trotters and all fried things, there is plenty from which to pick. I am fond of porridge and often make a lunch of it, cooked in milk with a tablespoon of soya flour and raw Bran.

Tripe, too, is easy on the tum, cooked in milk and mashed potatoes and a *small* onion. I like rice dishes, with kidney or as a pudding. Fish, mainly plaice, poached with parsley sauce, good steak cooked rare. Pancakes are jolly good, too, so is Shepherd's Pie. Eggs are a standby at all times, so is wholemeal bread and Flora.

I like tongue for breakfast and I have Orovit pills for Vits!

Chicken Pieces in Red Wine

Chicken pieces	
Red wine	
Pepper and salt	

Fold the chicken joints in foil parcels with salt and pepper and a little red wine. Steam with potatoes and greed!

A WEAK TUM's PRAYER

A bowl of porridge, a glass of milk & thou, in the WILDERNESS

Pitch

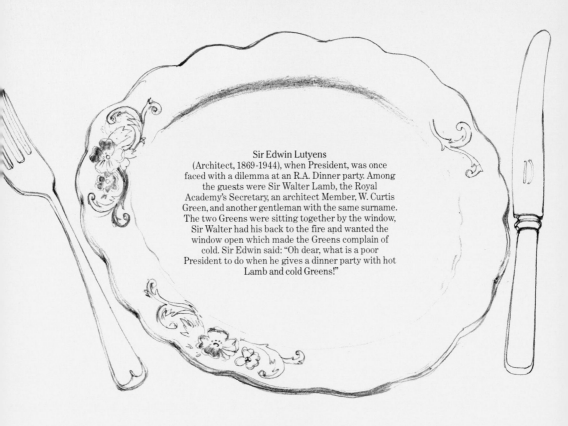

Sir Edwin Lutyens
(Architect, 1869-1944), when President, was once faced with a dilemma at an R.A. Dinner party. Among the guests were Sir Walter Lamb, the Royal Academy's Secretary, an architect Member, W. Curtis Green, and another gentleman with the same surname. The two Greens were sitting together by the window, Sir Walter had his back to the fire and wanted the window open which made the Greens complain of cold. Sir Edwin said: "Oh dear, what is a poor President to do when he gives a dinner party with hot Lamb and cold Greens!"

Chicken Curry

1 chicken cut into pieces	Juice of 1 lemon
1 finely chopped large onion	Salt to taste
2 cloves of garlic	
2 oz butter or oil	
½ tsp ground cumin seed	
½ tsp ground chillies	
1 tblsp of coriander	
1 tblsp dessicated coconut	
1 tsp ground turmeric	
½ tsp ground almonds	
½ pint sour milk (add lemon juice)	

Fry the onions and garlic in butter. Add all the ingredients except the milk and brown the chicken until golden brown colour.

Add the milk and put the ingredients into a casserole, place in oven on a low temperature. Cook slowly – flavour is increased by cooking the meal the day before and re-heating dish the next day. Serve with rice.

Ben Levene A.R.A.

Norman Blamey

R.A. 1975

Born: 1914. Studied: Polytechnic School of Art. Senior lecturer Chelsea School of Art 1963-1979. Works in private collections in UK and USA, and in permanent collections in S. Africa, USA and UK. Murals for Anglican Church of St Luke, Leagrave; Lutheran Church of St Andrew, Ruislip Manor.

I don't cook at all, my only experience of cooking was bully beef and biscuits in the war. It was the same thing you cooked each time but depending on the time of day it had a different name. It was either "biscuit burgoo" or "biscuit duff!"

I'm quite illogical over eating; I love cream, butter and cheese but if I get within smelling distance of a glass of milk, I feel nauseated. I loathe cream soups – if I get cream of mushroom when I'm out I have to gobble it quickly thinking hard of something else. Then, although I love butter, I read articles in magazines about cholesterol, and because I'm a coward and believe in being on the safe side, I don't eat butter or eggs but I haven't given up cream.

My tastes are very pedestrian and very English, and rarely meet with my wife's approval.

I think one's attitude towards food is as much psychological as physical; if as a child you are fed in a certain way you tend to continue in that way. I had a great passion for parsnips and ginger pudding as a child, now it would probably be smoked eel, steak and kidney pudding followed by something my mother used to make called Batchelor's Pudding – all stodge and by the time I'd finished all that I'd be incapable of moving!

Chicken Pie

Ingredients to serve six

Chicken (3 lbs)

Salt and pepper

Small peeled onion

Knob of herb butter e.g. parsley, mint and chives

2 rashers of bacon

½ pint of chicken stock (made from cube or giblet stock added to juice from chicken)

2 tblsp cornflour

1 oz of butter

Short crust pastry

6 oz self raising flour

4½ oz butter

Make the pastry by the rubbing in method, mix with a small amount of milk to a firm paste using a blunt ended knife.

Preparation Do not truss the bird. Season inside with salt and pepper and put in onion and herb butter. Insert the bacon rashers between the flesh and the skin – this keeps the breast moist. Cook slowly in a covered casserole dish for about 2 hours. At 275°/gas mark ½ – 1. Test by piercing the flesh, if the liquid runs out clear it is ready but if it is pink continue cooking. Pour the liquid in the dish into a basin to cool, remove fat and make it up to ½ pint with the stock. Pick the flesh from the bird while still warm, it should fall off the bone. Cut into bite size pieces and place in a pie dish. Blend 2 tablespoons cornflour with 1 oz of butter in a pan and gradually add the stock stirring until it thickens, then pour it over the chicken. The dish must be packed right up to the rim. Roll out pastry about ¼'thick and bigger than the size of the top of the pie dish. Cut strips of pastry long enough to go all round the dish. Damp the rim and stick them on. Damp the top of this and lift the large piece of pastry over without stretching it. Press the edge firmly and trim off surplus. Decorate with back of knife in scallop shapes. Bake at gas no. 6 for 25-30 mins or until golden brown.

Peter Coker

R.A. 1972

Born: 1926. Studied: St Martin's; RCA. Exhibited: Great Britain, Toronto, Austria.
Works in: Tate Gallery; Arts Council; CAS; Sheffield City Art Galleries;
National Portrait Gallery; Birmingham Art Gallery and numerous other public
collections.

I certainly look upon food as a pleasure. I don't cook myself, I do rather rely on other people to do it for me, though I'm not incapable of cooking if I have to.

I suppose there is a connection between painting and cooking. I know that when I was painting a lot of still lifes using all sorts of foods – hares and game and fish and so on, we used to eat the food afterwards and I think that's when I got interested in eating game. It was the painting that inspired the foods, not the other way round.

We always entertain at home, my wife's a *very* good cook. I'm rather loth to eat out in England, it's far too expensive.

A favourite meal? Oh, well, soups are an absolute favourite with me, then steak and kidney pie, so is chicken cooked in wine. I bring back vin ordinaire when we go to France. We cook a very good Lasagne too. I suppose a treat would be a nice plump pheasant or a poached salmon trout.

Chicken and White Wine Casserole

1 fresh chicken, skinned, cut into pieces and dipped into flour, seasoned with salt and black pepper.
1 or 2 carrots and onions
A clove or two of garlic roughly chopped
1 tsp mixed herbs and a bay leaf
Butter
½-1 pint white wine
1 pint stock

To make stock. Simmer for one hour the liver and neck of the chicken together with the mixed herbs in a pint of water. Reserve liquid and press liver through sieve with metal spoon. Season with salt and black pepper according to taste.

Melt butter over moderate heat in a deep casserole, add chopped carrots, onions and garlic, toss with wooden spoon until all are coated with butter. Add chicken pieces and simmer for 5-10 minutes turning constantly, pour in wine and leave to stand a few minutes, then add the stock, sieved liver and bay leaf (or two), cover and bring to simmering point, put casserole into pre-heated oven, Reg 4, 350°F for 1½-2 hours.

Serve with mashed potatoes, carrots or with any other root vegetable. A green pepper and/or a turnip may be added or substituted for the carrot/onion base. Follow with a caramel custard (see page 131).

Poulet Peck with red cabbage

1 3lb chicken

1 lemon

1 petit suisse

Handful of chopped fresh herbs

This is a good stand by for the working artist, it leaves you free for up to 3 hours.

The secret is the Roman Chicken "brick," an unglazed terracotta pot usually vaguely chicken shaped. Buy one from a potter at a sixth of the shop prices.

Defrost your chicken and cut off the parson's nose. Cut a lemon in half and massage the juice vigorously into the flesh. Pop a petit-suisse inside the carcass (keep the other two for the cheese board).

Now patinate with mixed herbs, put the liquid on and it's ready for the oven. No liquids or fats of any kind – it cooks in it's own juices. Cook at Reg. 4/350°F for 2 hours or so according to the instructions with the chicken brick.

It would be a poor economy not to utilise the same oven for a vegetable dish. I'm very fond of red cabbage in the winter months. Prepare it the night before to save studio daylight.

Red Cabbage

½ large red cabbage

2 chopped onions

2 red skinned apples

½ lb streaky bacon slices, rinds removed

2 tblsp Barbados sugar

Splash of cider vinegar

Handful of raisins

Salt and pepper

Take half a fair-size red cabbage. Shred it fine with a very sharp knife. You will need a nice oval casserole dish with a lid. Soften two chopped onions in boiling water and peel and core two red skinned apples, slice these neatly and uniformly.

Now layer upon layer, cabbage, onion, cabbage, apple, interspersed with generous rashers of streaky bacon, two tablespoons of Barbados raw sugar, a splash of cider vinegar, plus a handful of raisins and a little salt and pepper until you fill the casserole.

This can be left to cook very slowly and will be ready to serve with the chicken.

Complete the menu with fluffy, creamed potatoes and offer soured cream if available or parsley sauce if preferred.

Wash down with a glass of well chilled white burgundy.

David McFall R.A.

Pheasant à la Crème

1 tender pheasant
4 tblsp butter
2 tblsp olive oil
2 tblsp finely chopped carrot
2 tblsp finely chopped onion
Good pinch of thyme
1 crushed bay leaf
Salt and pepper
2-4 tblsp Cognac (heated)
½ pint double cream
Pheasant liver (cooked)
Butter
Cognac
Bread
Salt and freshly ground black pepper

Clean and truss pheasant and brown on all sides in butter and olive oil in flameproof casserole. Add finely chopped carrot and onion, thyme and bayleaf, season lightly. Cover casserole and simmer for 20 minutes. Pour off excess fat and flame with heated cognac. Moisten with cream; cover casserole with foil and lid and simmer until tender. Mash the pheasant liver with a little butter and Cognac and spread a canapé of white bread with this mixture. Remove bird; pass sauce through a fine sieve and correct seasoning. Place pheasant on the canapé and cover with sauce which should be quite thick. Serves four.

P.S. I do not usually pass the sauce through a sieve as we like the vegetable 'bits' in the sauce – also I only add a small amount of cream to moisten the casserole before simmering and add the rest of the cream to the sauce at the end when the bird has been removed and the remaining cream stirred into the sauce and heated up.

Ivor Roberts-Jones R.A.

MAIN COURSES
MEAT

Bryan Kneale

R.A. 1974

Born: 1930. Studied: Douglas School Art, (IOM); R.A. Schools; British School, Rome Scholar, 1949. Works in collections in: Australia, New Zealand, Canada, New York, Brazil, Tate and other London and provincial galleries.

I'm always accused of fantasizing over food rather than looking on it as sustenance. I'm drawn to rather odd or alarming things to eat. I like monkfish not only because it tastes quite good but it also has a terrifying head. I like entrails and brawn and odd bits and pieces, they have an element of danger about them.

I have a passion for fish and shellfish, I think it's because of their shapes. I love open air markets, particularly if they are near where there are Nigerians or Asians and you get all sorts of curious foods. My daughter has a friend who was brought up in India and we've all got very interested in Asian Cookery and all those peculiar spices.

I can cook but I tend to be over ambitious. It's the unexplored that interests me. I am nearly always inspired to start cooking at a late hour when half the ingredients aren't there and then I have to make concessions.

I do a lot of barbecuing, I have an amusing barbecue, it's an old blacksmith's forge. Whenever the sun's out we eat in the garden. In fact, when the sun's in, we still eat out. We're extremely hardy – though I do haul out my calor gas heaters and warm up the garden.

I once had an incredible meal in Scotland. I ordered steak and the waitress came and encased me in a large tartan bib, so I sat there feeling like an idiot. Eventually, the steak arrived, hissing and spitting on a lump of red hot granite! It was like being near a flame thrower! You could see the steak getting smaller and smaller, twitching away on the granite.

The only thing to do was to lever it on top of a wine glass to cool down. It was a meal of some interest and danger!

Scotch Haggis

Ingredients
Sheep's pluck and stomach
½ lb of suet
an onion
½ lb of oatmeal
pepper and salt

Have the stomach bag properly cleaned by the butcher, wash it well and put it in a saucepan of cold water and bring to the boil, which will make the bag contract. Take it out of the water at once, wash and scrape it well and lay it in salt and water. Wash the pluck thoroughly and boil it gently for one hour and a half with the windpipe hanging out over the edge of the pot so that all impurities may escape through it. Take all gristly parts from the lungs and heart, and mince the remainder, grate the best parts of the liver, chop the suet and onion fine, toast the oatmeal in the oven and put all in a basin with a dessertspoonful of salt and rather less than half the quantity of pepper. Moisten with half a pint of the liquor in which the pluck was boiled. Take the stomach bag from the brine and, keeping the smooth side inside, fill it with the mixture (not quite full) and sew it up. Put the haggis in a pot of boiling water and boil it gently for 3 hours, with a plate under to prevent it from sticking, and prick it now and then with a needle to prevent it bursting.

Time

3 hours to boil the haggis.

Michael Kenny

A.R.A. 1976

Born: 1941. Studied: Liverpool College of Art, Slade School. Sculptor. Exhibited
extensively in England, Europe, S. America, Australia. Work in Tate Gallery,
Arts Council and Public Collections in England and West Germany.

My biggest dislike are hard boiled eggs! I think that they are quite immoral. All that sulphur! I have a thing about boiled eggs. They are so seldom perfectly cooked. Everyone says "Oh, anyone can boil an egg" but it's quite difficult, they vary so much according to size and freshness and one can't see inside till it's too late!

All the best cooks I know operate on an intuitive basis. It's one thing repeating a recipe from a book but most really good cooks play it by ear. If you ask them how they do it, they are at a loss to tell you.

I wouldn't call myself a cook. I can make a reasonable Bolognese sauce and the usual sort of fry-ups. I often have a huge mixed grill for breakfast on Sundays which I cook up myself. I'd like to be able to cook really well but I haven't the time. I rather fancy Chinese cookery. I bought myself a Chinese cookbook but I haven't got round to using it yet. I like the idea of the speed with which it's done – fry it in 30 seconds in one of those special round bottomed pans.

I like eating on trains, it helps to while away the journey and is an indulgence. For Birthday treats we'd eat at home for my birthday, but my wife, Angela is a professional cook and for her's I'd take her out! What would I choose? Well, my big thing is snails. I once ate four plates of them. Yes, I did feel a bit funny afterwards! I rather over indulged in escargots! But still I order them if they are on the menu.

Scouse

1 lb shin beef (originally mutton)
1 large Spanish onion
3 carrots
½ turnip
1 cube of beef extract in 1 pint of water (originally plain water) can also include (though not originally) a sprinkling of mixed herbs with an extra pinch of thyme.
4 very large potatoes (or equivalent in smaller potatoes)
Salt and pepper to taste

When considering a recipe for the cookbook, it seemed appropriate that I should choose SCOUSE, partly because it is the traditional dish of my native Liverpool and partly because the recipe rarely appears in books. The recipe I have given here is that which was cooked often by my mother and which I remember as a child. Essentially scouse is a derivative of Irish stew and like Irish stew was originally a poverty dish; unlike Irish stew, though, it should be cooked until it is a thick sludge – it is said that one should be able to put one's fork into a plate of scouse and that the fork should remain vertical. There was an original variation of scouse (for those who could not afford meat) known as 'lobscouse' or 'blindscouse' this was simply stewed vegetables without meat and more or less any vegetable that was at hand could be thrown in, lobscouse was eaten in

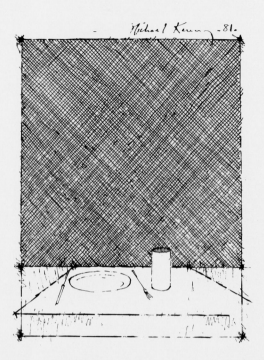

Liverpool during the rationing of the 2nd World War. An essential addition to scouse is the 'swag', this traditionally consists of pickled beetroot, pickled red cabbage or pickled onion or raw onion or any combination of these. As a drink to take with scouse, I recommend a pint of 'black & tan' (a bottle of Guinness mixed with good draught bitter).

Method:- Dice the meat into 1 inch cubes and fry in a little oil or fat for about 2 minutes, drain the fat and put the meat into a stewing pan – then add the onion, carrots and turnip (sliced) beef extract mixed in 1 pint of hot water, herbs and seasoning. Bring this to the boil and then simmer for two hours, the meat should now be well cooked and softened – then add the potato diced 1″ square approx. (this should absorb most of the liquid) one could also, at this stage add 1 teaspoonful of gravy browning mixed in a very small amount of water. Continue to cook until the scouse becomes a thick sludge – stirring constantly to prevent the scouse sticking to the pan. If preferred, the scouse could then be put into an oven dish and covered with pastry and baked in the oven.

To savour the full delights of scouse, it should be liberally covered with swag – my own preference is sliced beetroot and onion both pickled in malt vinegar for about half an hour before eating.

William Brooker

A.R.A. 1980

Born: 1918. Studied: Croydon and Chelsea Schools of Art. Work in permanent collections: Tate and other British provincial galleries; National Galleries Canada, New Zealand, South Australia; Museum of Modern Art, Belo Horisonte, Brazil.

"Is food a pleasure or just fuel?"

Oh, it's a *JOY!* I really like everything. I love grilled sole, and duck in any form – particularly if someone else is paying the bill! I like highly flavoured things, lots of garlic and spices – garlic in everything – except tea!

My wife is Peruvian and although there's no "Peruvian Cuisine" we do have a Peruvian cookery book with a recipe that starts: "Take a live rabbit and cut it's head off with a sharp knife"! We don't do that one too often.

I've always cooked, I like it. I think many artists are interested in cooking, it's similar to painting – you take raw materials and turn them into something else.

I'm a great tea drinker. I have to have at least a pint of tea and a cigarette before I can put a foot out of bed.

Do we have "tea, supper or dinner?" I suppose we have something called "a meal"! What would I choose? Oh – (does cost matter?) Well, then Beluga Caviar, Tripe à la Mode de Caen (but I'd have to go to Caen to eat it, you can't get the right tripe here), and a bit of Brie to finish.

Sauté de Veau

6 veal escalopes, flattened very thin (or a similar quantity of pork fillet, cut into thin rounds and flattened between 2 sheets of greaseproof paper with a wooden rolling-pin)

Seasoned flour

2-3 ozs of (preferably) clarified butter

½ pint of chicken stock

½ pint dry white wine

½ lb thinly sliced mushrooms

Sherry glass of Malmsey

¼ pint double cream

Chopped parsley

Flour the escalopes and shake off surplus. Heat the butter in a sauté pan and sauté the escalopes gently, turning them from time to time, for about ten minutes. Put them on crumpled kitchen paper to drain and keep warm.

Scrape up the pan juices with a wooden scraper while adding the stock and wine a bit at a time. Add the mushrooms and reduce the sauce over a high heat, stirring and scraping constantly until the sauce has thickened. Add the malmsey and boil for a few more moments, remove from heat and add the cream, stirring it in gradually. Season lightly.

Pour over the escalopes, sprinkle with chopped parsley and serve.

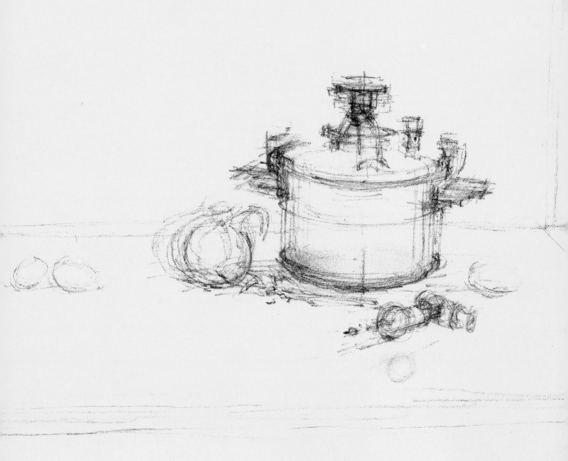

John Partridge

A.R.A. 1980

John Partridge ARA, FRIBA, was born in 1924 and studied at the Polytechnic School
of Architecture, Regent Street qualifying as an architect in 1951. In 1959 with his
partners he founded the architectural practice of Howell Killick Partridge & Amis,
which is based in Westminster and known for its university work and for public and
educational buildings. (He has served as Vice President of the Royal Institute of British
Architects from 1977-79 and has been its Honorary Librarian for four years.
He is presently an external examiner in achitecture at Cambridge University and
Thames Polytechnic.) C.B.E. 1981

I have a standard breakfast that everyone laughs at – a small bowl of bran, a banana, some honey and milk. Lunch is a sandwich and a glass of beer. My eating is mainly in the evening. I suppose my favourite dish is veal escalope and spaghetti and I do have a weakness for Crepes Suzettes. I like Hungarian Goulash, I think nearly every country has its own sort of stew, goulash, curry, Irish stew, all cheap nourishing foods; there's a whole range of them and they are all good.

Yes, I have designed kitchens. I think they should be large and designed as a specific type of *living* room. My kitchen at home is quite efficient. It's got plenty of space to eat in and it's near the dining room, so food doesn't get cold. It's also near the sitting rooms if you want to take food in to watch TV. The one thing I would have liked in the kitchen is an outside door, but my house is a listed building so we can't break through walls.

I've designed kitchens for big establishments too, their size depends not only on the number of people that have to be catered for but also on the range of dishes on the menu needing large pieces of equipment.

Veal Escalope Milanese (with spaghetti)

Serves 4

Milanese Tomato Sauce

14 oz can peeled plum tomatoes

1 tblsp of oil

1 small onion, chopped

1 carrot, chopped

Stick of celery, chopped

½ garlic clove, crushed

Salt and freshly ground black pepper

1 tsp basil or oregano

Warm the oil in a pan then add chopped onion, carrot, celery and crushed garlic and fry until brown. Add sieved plum tomatoes, salt and pepper and basil or oregano and simmer for at least 30 minutes.

Spaghetti Push the spaghetti into a large pan of *boiling* salted water and stir until water reboils. Boil uncovered for about 10-12 minutes or until just tender (al dente). Tip into a colander, then rinse under running cold water. Drain well. Return to the rinsed out pan and heat gently with one tablespoon of olive oil, turning carefully with wooden spoon. Place spaghetti in a warmed serving dish with the escalope and pour over milanese sauce. Serve with grated Parmesan cheese sprinkled on top of the sauce.

Veal

8 veal escalopes, preferably from the noix (the best part of the leg) or from the loin or neck.

2 eggs

Salt and freshly ground pepper

Bread crumbs

1 oz butter

While the spaghetti is cooking beat the eggs with salt and pepper. Put the veal first into the egg and then into the bread crumbs. In a frying pan over a moderate heat melt the butter. When the butter is foaming fry the escalopes for 3-4 minutes on each side until a very delicate brown. Take out the veal with a perforated spoon or fish slice and keep warm in a very low oven.

Joseph Nollekens
(Sculptor, 1737-1823) was noted for his parsimonious habits, anything to save a penny or two. He would even pocket the nutmegs from the table at R.A. dinners.

James Barry
(Painter, 1741-1806) had the curious habit when visiting friends of leaving money on the table to pay for his food. He didn't care to be "beholden to them for anything except the conversation and company." He wouldn't dine with a friend without leaving two shillings on the cloth – no matter what the hospitality. He used to go to tea with Stubbs on condition that he paid sixpence each time.

KITCHEN
THINGS.

J.D.

Jennifer Dickson

R.A. 1976

Born: 1936. Freelance graphic artist and photographer. Lives in Canada.
Studied: Goldsmith's; Atelier 17, Paris. French Govt. Scholarship to work under
S. W. Hayter in Paris. Directed and developed: Printmaking Dept., Brighton;
Graphics Atelier, Saidye Bronfman Centre, Montreal.
Awarded Prix de Jeunes Artistes (Gravure), Paris Biennale 1963. Lives in Canada.

I hate complicated cooking – things with lots of sauces. The sort of food I like best is the simple food we used to eat in Paris when I was studying with Hayter. We'd buy a stick of French bread and half a pound of pâté and cheese and some olives and a bottle of wine. My favourite dishes are very simple and unpretentious, but my greatest love is Indian food. My mother sometimes sends me spices and different curries from South Africa. For very special friends, who really know what they are eating, I cook curries. I make three or four and it takes me most of a day. Then I let them stand for a few days to mature. I can't serve curries to Canadians, they have such bland palate.

We entertain a lot, either small dinner parties or huge lavish studio parties, nothing between! I now have large parties down to an art, we have two or three a year. I have a barman and two waitresses and serve a buffet supper of pâtés and salads and cheeses and French bread. If we have a dinner party we often have fresh salmon which we can still get fairly reasonably in Canada. If I want to honour someone very special I get a whole smoked salmon. I did that when Sir Hugh came over last year.

I run an enormous house and being an artist and a teacher I try not to spend too long a time in the kitchen. All our meals are of things I can get on to the table in 30 minutes – steaks and grilled lamb chops – steak is still inexpensive in Canada. We always have a stock pot and we make a lot of soups in winter. My favourite meal is breakfast – traditional bacon and eggs!

Ground Beef and Bean Sprouts

3 Spanish onions
2 tablespoons butter
2 cloves of garlic, chopped finely
¼ lb mushrooms (sliced) – optional
1 lb lean ground beef
1 lb fresh bean sprouts
½ lb long grain rice
Genuine mushroom soya sauce

This is my son, William David's, favourite recipe. Quantities vary, depending on number. This is for 3 people.

Steam rice separately. Slice onions and brown in covered frying pan with 2 tablespoons butter. Brown beef. Add garlic then ⅓ cup soya sauce. Cover, and simmer for 8 minutes on low heat. 3 minutes before serving, place mushrooms and bean sprouts on top of ground beef; cover pan, and steam briefly on high heat. Serve on bed of rice. Additional soya sauce may be added to taste. Do not overcook the bean sprouts, they should be crisp.

Pork Chops Bloomsbury

Serves 2 hungry souls

4 pork chops

1 x 5 fl oz bottle Soy sauce

1 large onion sliced

½ clove of garlic or granules

Plus extra herbs you may fancy such as tarragon, oregano or rosemary

Black pepper

Select your pork chops carefully. They should be cut from the loin; if not available, cutlets will do. Place them in a bowl of soy sauce for at least half an hour. Place the pork chops on a bed of onion slices in a casserole or roasting tin. Sprinkle with chopped garlic or granules, the chosen herbs, a little rosemary and black pepper.

Place the casserole or roasting tin just below the centre in a moderately hot oven (Gas 5, 375°F) and leave for one hour.

Serve with a dry flakey rice and consume with a bottle of light dry red wine, i.e. a Chianti Classico or Rioja.

Paul Hogarth A.R.A.

Saltimbocca
Literally "Jump in the Mouth"

2 or 3 slices veal per person (hammered as thinly as possible)

2 or 3 slices of raw or cooked ham

Fresh sage leaves

Salt and pepper

Butter

Small glassful Marsala or white wine

Place a slice of ham and one fresh sage leaf onto each flattened slice of veal. Make into a roll and secure with a toothpick. Season and gently fry in butter till browned. Add a small glassful of Marsala or white wine and allow to bubble for one minute. Cover pan and simmer till meat is cooked (10-15 mins).

Delicious served with croûtons. Beef thinly sliced may also be used but the cooking takes slightly longer.

Sidney C. Hutchison
SECRETARY

Peter Greenham
R.A. 1960

Born: 1909. Studied: Byam Shaw School. Keeper R.A. Schools since 1964.
Published work on Velasquez. C.B.E. 1978

95

Carbonnade of Beef

1½ lb chuck steak
2 onions
1 clove garlic
2 tblsp dripping
1 tblsp flour
½ pint brown ale
1 pint hot water
Bouquet Garni
Salt and pepper
Pinch of grated nutmeg
Pinch of sugar
1 tsp vinegar
2 slices of bread
French mustard

Cut meat into large squares, slice the onions, chop and crush garlic with a little salt. Heat dripping in a stewpan, when smoking, brown the meat quickly on both sides. Lower gas and add onions, dust on the flour, pour on ale and water, add garlic, bouquet garni and season with salt, pepper, nutmeg, sugar and vinegar. Stir until boiling, turn into oven-proof casserole, cover and cook slowly on 325°/reg 3 for about 2½-3 hours.

Remove crust from bread, 40 minutes before serving, take out bouquet garni, skim-off any fat and leave uncovered.

Lay slices of bread on top and push down firmly, smother with french mustard and return casserole to oven uncovered.

Cook for rest of time until the bread forms a good brown crust.

Ben Levene A.R.A.

Lamb Casserole

1½-2 lbs lean pieces of lamb (i.e. the long piece which is cut from a shoulder of lamb and called fillet)
The same amount of carrots and onions
2 oz fat or oil
3 tblsp flour
1 pint of stock or water
Bay leaf and seasoning

This is my favourite lamb casserole.

Cut the lamb in pieces (there is no fat on this type of fillet). Melt fat in casserole – one of those that can also go on top of stove – and stir in flour cooking until it turns yellow. Add liquid and mix well. Add the other ingredients and cook in oven very slowly until tender – 2 or more hours.

Olwyn Bowey R.A.

Robert Clatworthy

R.A. 1973

Born: 1928. Sculptor. Studied: West of England College Art; Chelsea School; Slade.
Exhibited: Tate, British Sculpture in the Sixties 1965. Works in:
Tate; Arts Council; CAS; V & A; GLC.

I do all my own cooking, actively enjoying the process. I usually need to produce meals quickly and since I can't spare the time to shop around, rely on what I can get locally. I use a pressure cooker a great deal since it cuts time to a minimum. It's useful for fish, meat and vegetables, not only soups and stews.

My main meal is supper which I have at any time between 6.00 and 10.00, often missing lunch altogether. I almost never eat out now because I'd far rather buy a couple of decent bottles of wine than pay restaurant prices. It may be more *amusing* to have a meal out but the food is seldom better. Occasionally, if it's a serious business meeting about work, it may be easier to take people out, but I don't normally find that cooking gets in the way of entertaining.

A favourite meal? I'd start with snails and then a very rare fillet steak and a fairly complicated salad and a nice bottle of Lafitte, cheese and fruit.

The one thing I really hate are pickled onions and I'm allergic to oysters.

Lamb under Pressure

Oil
Large sliced Spanish onion
Sliced parsnip
Garlic
Bay leaf
3 peppercorns
Salt and pepper
4 to 6 pieces neck of mutton
Rosemary
3 or 4 potatoes

A little oil in the pressure cooker, then add onion, parsnip, garlic and bay leaf. Sauté till soft with peppercorns, salt and pepper. Add neck of mutton, generously sprigged with rosemary and cook quickly to seal. Add the onions, bring to pressure. Cook for 20 minutes. Slice potatoes and lay on top. Bring to pressure for about 10 minutes, and that's it.

Interesting because it's so easy and you can vary it in all kinds of ways. I never follow a recipe slavishly. Serve with rosemary jelly and a crisp salad.

Carel Weight

R.A. 1965

Born: 1908. Studied: Hammersmith School Art; Goldsmith's. Official War Artist.
Prof. Painting School, RCA. Exhibited England and abroad. C.B.E.1961

I look upon food as one of the great pleasures of life. I enjoy food enormously and of course, drink too, But I wouldn't say I was a toper! I do like really good wine.

Do I cook? No, only in a very, very small way. I'm not a cook, I look upon it as one of those wonderful mysteries that other people do for me. Cooking should be creative and I think it is surprising that such a large number of artists whose work I admire, I can also admire as cooks. They approach it in a slightly intuitive way which really is the secret of their success.

Mine is a very negative breakfast: I only have coffee, unless I'm paying an enormous amount staying in a hotel, then I take advantage of it! I don't stop work in my studio for elevenses but I'm really rather hungry by lunchtime, so I like to go out for lunch, to get away from the studio and have a real break. Then I come back and see my work with a fresh eye.

A favourite meal? I don't like lots of courses of tiny little things. I think three courses are about right. I quite like artichokes with vinaigrette, and, oh, there are so many things I like, roast duck and some very nice Stilton or French cheese. If you asked me *now* to name my unfavourite things, I'd be very hard put to it, I mean, unseasoned tough meat, or badly under cooked fish, of course one hates it, but otherwise I really like everything. I like looking at cookery books, they're intriguing, not only for recipes but they are often very nicely laid out and you get lovely illustrations of luscious foods.

Lamb Pilaff

½ lb rice	2 tblsp roasted and ground poppy seeds
1¼ lb lamb (cut into pieces)	2 bay leaves
2 limes	¼ cup of jellied stock
8 ground aniseed/fennel seeds	Salt
¼ pint lightly whipped double cream	6 tblsp chopped spinach or watercress
Carton of natural yoghurt	
4 oz clarified butter	
4 cloves	
7 bruised cardamoms	
Cinnamon stick – 2″ long	

Soak the rice in cold water for an hour and then drain. Remove any skin from the lamb then prick the pieces all over and rub in the lime juice and aniseed or fennel. Mix the cream and yoghurt, put the lamb pieces in the mixture and set aside.

Heat some of the butter and add the cloves and stock. Stir, then cover and leave on a low heat for 5 minutes. In another pan heat the remaining butter with the cardamoms, cinnamon, poppy seed and bay leaves. Add the rice and cook over a medium heat for 6 or 8 minutes, stirring occasionally. Remove the meat from the cream and yoghurt mixture. Add the mixture and stock to the pan of rice so that it is covered by approx. 1¼" of liquid. Bring to the boil then add salt and chopped watercress or spinach. Steam for a few minutes.

Fry the meat until crisp and brown and put in the middle of the rice, then heap the rice on top of the meat. Place in a low oven for 15 minutes then remove and garnish with any of the following: onion rings dipped in batter and fried, raisins (which have been soaked and drained) lightly fried, pimento rings either roasted or grilled or almonds which have been blanched, slivered and fried.

John Ward

R.A. 1965

Born: Hereford 1917. Studied: Hereford Art School, R.C.A. 1939-46. Royal Engineers R.C.A.
Travelling scholarship 1947. 1948-52 worked for Vogue. A.R.A. 1956. Portrait
painter, book illustrator and architectural draughtsman.

Food is everything to the painter, sustenance & subject from mother's milk to the last supper.

So many painters raided the kitchen, Chardin must have spent half his life with one eye on what was cooking, what was being cooked and who was cooking. The utensils of the kitchen seem more popular with the painter than the porcelain of the boudoir. In our own day John Bratby has immortalized the corn flakes box but I have yet to see the Kenwood take its place in the cosy tradition.

All painters must be able to do two things at once, eat and observe, drink and note. meal times are the most natural gatherings of human beings plus splendid still life therefore it follows that a painter must be, if not the cook's right hand man, at least the cook's most eager & appreciative client.

Shrewdly, the Royal Academy has always made much of dinners and lunches; its handsome rooms and historic silver and lust for good food & wine has always attracted the wit, nobility and famous of the nation. And how sensible to have made feasting an essential part of the artist's life

100

Spicy Roast Lamb

Leg of lamb
½ pint yoghurt
2 cloves garlic
2″ fresh root ginger, peeled and finely chopped
6 cardamom pods
1½ tsp ground cumin
½ tsp turmeric powder
Rosemary
2 lbs potatoes
¾lb onions peeled and very thinly sliced
Salt and pepper
1 pint stock
1 oz butter (melted) or 2 tblsp oil

Make incisions in the leg of lamb and insert garlic in little bits. Make a marinade of the yoghurt, ginger, cardamoms, cumin and turmeric and cover the lamb with this overnight.

Next day lay the lamb on some sprigs of rosemary in a large roasting tin surrounded by a bed of thinly sliced potatoes and onions in alternating layers well seasoned. Pour over the boiling stock and the melted butter over the lamb (or oil). Roast in moderately hot oven 190°C/ 375°F Reg 5 allowing 30 mins to the lb.

Anthony Eyton

A.R.A. 1976

Born: 1923. Studied: Camberwell School of Art. Awarded Abbey Major Scholarship to Italy. Member London Group. Head of Painting Department, St. Lawrence, Ontario. Teaches at Camberwell and R.A. schools. Work in public collections in this country. Restrospective Exhibition: South London Gallery, Towner Art Gallery, Eastbourne, Plymouth Art Gallery.

I'm interested in survival, so yes, I do cook for myself. I rather like boiled carrots just by themselves! I'm really far more interested in painting and getting on with my work, so I don't go looking in cookery books to find something to cook when I have people. I just get a bit of beef, that is nice and simple to do, not a lot of fiddle.

I think breakfast is important, I usually have cereal, toast and tea and maybe an orange. I can't take coffee at breakfast time, it makes me jumpy. At that time in the morning it speeds things up too much, it's as if the engine's going round too fast. I'd like to try herb teas but I haven't got round to it yet.

I usually have a salad, bread and cheese and an apple for lunch. I suppose you'll go and quote this but I do find it advantageous to have a little nap after meals, just half an hour to get out of the world!

If I invite people, I ask them to "supper," but if I'm going out, I go "out to dinner." I suppose it's not making too important a thing out of asking people – "dinner" sounds a bit pompous! The difference is all very subtle!

A favourite meal? Oh, Italian ham and melon, steak or salmon instead of steak and afterwards any sort of pudding. Cookery books make a good bedtime reading – very relaxing! I can't do many dishes, that's why I chose meat balls. Its a rough and ready simple thing.

Meat Balls

1 lb of minced meat (½ lb of best lean minced beef and ½ lb of minced veal is suggested)	1 glass of wine
	Parsley
½ cup of fresh breadcrumbs	small pot of yoghurt or soured cream
1 egg	
1 tsp of thyme	
½ tsp of salt	
black pepper	
2 tblsps of olive oil	
2 onions, finely chopped	
clove of garlic	
½ tsp of basil	
2 x 8 oz tin of plum tomatoes	
Lemon juice or zest	

Mix the breadcrumbs, egg and mince with a fork in a bowl. Add thyme, salt and pepper. Shape the meat balls no larger than a large walnut, and fry in olive oil for about 12 minutes, until crisp, at medium heat turning occasionally.

Meanwhile fry the onions and then put in the tomatoes, basil, garlic and wine and simmer for 20 minutes. Pour over meat balls, garnish with parsley and serve with rice and soured cream/ yoghurt.

Anthony Eyton

Sir Frederick Gibberd

R.A. 1969

Frederick Gibberd is the only architect to have designed a Cathedral, a Mosque,
and a non-conformist Chapel and a Monastry and is likely to remain so. As a Town
Planner his best known work is Harlow New Town.
In 1977 he received the Gold Medal of the Royal Town Planning Institute
"for outstanding achievement in the field of town and country planning." C.B.E.
1954 Kt 1967

For me cooking is either a fine art – haute cuisine, or a craft – regional home cooking. In between it is merely serving up food.

I am addicted to exploring unfamiliar urban scenes and part of the process includes the luxuries of five-star hotels – (a reaction to a non-conformist background) – luxuries, which include quiet, a discreet staff, a Head Porter who finds tickets for the opera that is sold out, elegant guests seemingly unaware of wealth, a vast bathroom with clean towels every day and original cooking served in a distinguished ambience – the Gritti Palace, Venice, the San Dominico, Taormina, the Villa Igila, Palermo, the George V, Paris, the Mamunia, Marrakesh, to name, at random, the scene of some fabulous holidays.

The chefs at grand hotels have their speciality and there are those worth seeking out for particular dishes: the Inter-Continental, Hyde Park Corner for soufflés, the Howard, Temple Place for oeuf en cocotte with bone marrow, incidentally both hotels were designed by me except for the Adam decor of the latter. Further afield the Villa Condulmar Venezia for incomparable pasta, the Domino Peregeux for truffles with everything! – such gastronomical excursions can be endless.

My appreciation of regional home cooking is solely due to my grandmother who also introduced me to another art, that of garden design. As a small boy I frequently ran away from home – not surprisingly with four young brothers and a harassed mother. No one was concerned for they knew I

had gone to "Granny Nuneaton," a cycle-ride from my home in Coventry, there to be welcomed with warmth, affection and a larder loaded with home cooking. In that larder, a large room, was half a pig curing in brine in a stone trough. All was eaten: fabulous roasts with surfeits of crackling, ham, bacon, trotters, scratchings and home-made brawn, pork pies and sausages. Cooking, alas, that I can now only experience in imagination.

My grandmother also introduced me to another culinary

delight, tripe brought back from the butchers in a jug ready soaked and boiled. She then steamed it with milk, onion and butter. Served with mashed potatoes it can be delicious, but overcooked it becomes a disgusting slithering mess. The Étoile in Charlotte Street do it exactly as my grandmother did, although they call it Tripe à la Normandie and she never went further than Bournemouth.

In my pursuance of the art of town design I collect piazzas – drawing and photographing them. Finding Florence infested with motorcars, Germans and French schoolgirls all called Yvonne bent on seeing the Botticellis, we went to explore other towns and cities. Of these Siena was the most memorable, not because of the piazza which is too loose an open space but because in it was to be found a small restaurant which served Trippa alla Fiorentina. Italian tripe is from veal more delicate than the English ox. It is cooked in freshly-made tomato sauce, seasoned with marjoram and stewed with a thick layer of Parmesan cheese before serving – Elizabeth David has the recipe.

Incidentally I cannot cook and have no desire to do so. As a widower I lived on lobster bisque and pâté picked up from Fortnums after leaving Burlington House.

Tristram Hillier

R.A. 1971

Born: 1905. Painter and writer. Studied: Slade School; under Andre Lhote, Paris.
Works in public collections: Tate; Australia; Canada; Belfast; England.
Publication: Leda and the Goose, autobiography, 1954.

I appreciate good food but I love wine more. I cannot cook but during the first year of my marriage I engaged a 'Cordon Bleu' at my house in Normandy. She was extremely expensive but it proved to be the wisest investment of my life for my wife consequently became one of the best cooks I have ever known.

Of the many great meals I have enjoyed in various countries I think one of the most remarkable was a luncheon party given by my old friend George Rainbird in honour of André Simon's eightieth birthday. It was remarkable not for the food, which was simple, but the perfection of really good English cooking to which there can be no better complement than fine wines.

It was remarkable for the glorious wines.

Much as I enjoy French cooking it is often too rich to set off a delicate wine. Here then was our menu:

Moët et Chandon, Dom Pérignon 1943
Jerez Viejissimo 1770
    Game Soup
Bâtard Montrachet 1945
    Sweetbread Soufflé
Château Latour 1934 (Magnum)
    Saddle of Whichford Lamb
Château Ausone 1924 (Magnum)
    Saddle of Whichford Lamb
Château Haut Brion 1920 (Magnum)
    Tomes aux Raisins
    Brie, Gruyere.
Château Mouton Rothschild 1877
(This wine, the year of André

Simon's birth, was sent by the Baron Luis de Rothschild from his private cellar).
Cheese as above
Hennessy Grande Fine Champagne 1913
    Dessert

We sat down to lunch at one o'clock and rose from the table at five.

George Rainbird had said to me beforehand: "I am inviting you to this luncheon on condition that you take away all the empty bottles and paint a large 'Bottle-scape' for my dining room." This I did and it was the most enjoyable commission of my life. It was exhibited at the Royal Academy in 1958 and now hangs in George Rainbird's dining room in the Albany.

stalk and fry in fat. Place the fried vegetables in bottom of roasting pan, put the leg on top and roast, basting with melted lard and a little stock. When the meat is done, pass gravy and vegetables through colander, season gravy and serve separately in sauce-boat. Surround the leg with different kinds of cooked beans— haricots verts, broadbeans and baked beans.

Gulyás (Beef stew, Hungarian style)

This famous dish is quite simple to make and yet it is seldom correctly prepared when not cooked by a native of Hungary. For 6 persons allow 2½ to 3 lbs. boneless beef, trim off all fat and cut into 2 in. pieces. Melt in heavy pan 2 tablespoons lard and fry first 3 large sliced onions and when the onions begin to wilt, stir in ½ tablespoon Hungarian rose-paprika. Add now the meat —which should be washed and drained but not dried— and brown the pieces on all sides over medium heat (do not fry too quickly). Season with salt and pepper and a pinch of chopped caraway-seeds. Wash and cut up 3 or 4 large, ripe tomatoes and add to stew (tomato-paste may be used instead). Add just a little stock to begin with, cover and simmer for 2 hours, adding stock if necessary; the meat should be barely covered by gravy. Before serving add 2 lbs. cooked, peeled and quartered potatoes (the pink, firm sort), mixing well into gravy.

Gyuvetch (Serbian stew)

The name of this delicious dish is pronounced "Dioowetch". Cut into neat pieces 2 lbs. boneless pork

73

Mince with Onions

"Proper mince is good put in the oven with milk,
and a few small cooked onions so that it becomes like lean steak, with tomatoes.**"**
Craigie Aitchison A.R.A.

Sir John Millais
(Painter, 1829-1896) was one of the youngest and most
gifted students at the Royal Academy Schools in the
1840s. Because he was the smallest and youngest he
was expected to fag for the others. "I was told off by
the other students to obtain for them their lunch. I had
to collect 40 or 50 pennies from my companions and
go with that hoard to a neighbouring Baker's and
purchase the same number of buns. It generally
happened that I got a bun myself by way of
commission!"

Steak and Kidney Pudding

Meat
1-1½ lb stewing steak, chuck or shin
4-6 kidneys
Flour
Salt and pepper
¼ pint water or stock

Pastry
8 oz self raising flour
1 tsp salt
4 oz shredded suet
7/8 tblsp water

For this recipe you will need a large saucepan, half filled with water, a 1½ pint size basin (greased) and well greased foil or greaseproof paper for the pudding cover.

Cut steak and kidney into small pieces. Toss in dry bowl with flour, salt and pepper. Make pastry, soft not sticky. Cut off ⅓rd for top of pudding.

Roll out remainder to line basin, fill with floured meat, then water or stock halfway up. Damp edge of pastry all round. Roll out the ⅓rd of pastry for top of pudding, and cover it with same.

Cover the completed pudding with greased paper or foil, I use foil. Make pleat across the middle to allow for rising. Tie foil around the basin with string, making a handle across the top to allow for lifting now and then, add hot water to pan which must not dry up.

Water must not come up too high to touch top of pudding. Finally cover with saucepan lid. Keep this simmering for 4/5 hours the longer the better for a light brown crusty suet, or 3/4 hours will suffice for a well cooked pudding.

Walter Woodington
CURATOR, ROYAL ACADEMY SCHOOLS

Liver in Cream

50 grams of butter
1 medium onion sliced
200 grams of mushrooms sliced (leave stalks out)
350 grams lambs liver cut into strips
150 millilitres double cream

The liver should be soaked in milk overnight (just enough to cover it).

Melt butter and cook onions in it taking care that they don't brown. Add mushrooms and cook until soft (5 mins). Remove from pan, put on one side and keep warm.

Put the liver in the pan (without the milk) and cook until soft 8-10 mins. Return the onions and mushrooms to the pan. Cover and leave on a low heat. Retire for an aperitif and first course. Return and stir in the cream and salt and pepper to taste. Heat the cream till warm (don't boil) and serve with boiled rice.

Stephen Rees-Jones
PROFESSOR OF CHEMISTRY

Rich Rabbit Casserole

1 rabbit cut in pieces	Wineglass of red wine (optional)
4 ozs streaky bacon	
18 small onions	
2 ozs butter	
1½ oz flour	
1 pint stock	
Bouquet garni	
4 cloves	
6 peppercorns	
Seasoning	

Dice bacon, and peel onions. Brown onions and bacon in butter and set on one side. Fry rabbit in the same butter until lightly browned, add flour and continue frying until well browned. Replace bacon and onions, add hot stock, bouquet garni, cloves, peppercorns. Season and cover. Simmer for 1½ hours in oven or until rabbit is tender. Add red wine about 10 minutes before serving. Serve at once.

Patricia Libby
FRIENDS OFFICE

Pork cooked in Milk

Pork in a roll (without skin) or pork fillets
Onions
Clove of garlic
Slice of ham or rashers of bacon
Butter or olive oil
Coriander seeds
Fennel seeds
Basil
Pint of milk
Salt and black pepper

Chop onions finely, crush garlic, cube ham or bacon and gently soften in the butter or oil in a large pan. Season the pork. Sprinkle with coriander seeds, fennel seeds and basil and lightly seal in the pan with the onions and ham. Meanwhile bring the milk to almost boiling point and then pour over the pork. Allow to simmer, keeping the lid off, so that the liquid reduces. Fine layers of skin will form over the meat. Do not disturb this for the first ¾ hour of cooking. When the liquid has reduced to approx. one cupful stir well to avoid sticking. This stage must be watched as the liquid evaporates rapidly. A creamy liquid will have formed which makes the sauce.

Lesley Woodbridge
LIBRARY

MAIN COURSES
Vegetarian

Sir Richard Sheppard

R.A. 1972

Born: 1910. Studied: RWA and AA Schools of Architecture.
Principal commissions: City Univ., London; Brunel Univ., Uxbridge;
Churchill College, Cambridge (competition); and other educational and commercial
buildings. Vice-Pres. RIBA, 1969-70. Published works on architecture.
C.B.E. 1964, Kt. 1981

I like *all* kinds of food, I can't think of anything I *don't* like. But though a carnivore, I always prefer vegetables of all kinds, particularly the less usual ones. They *must* be properly cooked not overcooked.

I like the cuisines of almost all the countries I've been to, I can even put up with Greece and Finland which I think are the worst. The best cuisine is North Italian – anything North of Rome, and of course, good French cooking. Turkish too is very good.

I think cooking is creative, yes, emphatically cooking is an art. All good cooks are inventive, but the trouble is that it depends so much on cheap or committed labour. The reason why French cooking has gone down so much lately is because French-women are no longer prepared to spend most of the day preparing a soup, it's the same with the restaurants.

No, I don't cook but we always discuss the menu and the ingredients and I usually prepare one course when we have someone coming, but my wife does the main course which demands the oven because I can't get things out from a wheelchair.

A favourite meal: to start Ricotta con Spinaci and a main course of Turbot Dieppoise with Fennel and if I have a sweet (I never take sweets) but the one I like best is a Pot au Chocolat and if one was going to have cheese it would be Roquefort. I can only afford to drink slop! I think I like a Burgundy best.

Finally, I was brought up to eat what was put in front of me, and I still do.

Gnocchi Alla Fiorentina

2 lbs spinach	
1 oz flour	
2 oz butter	
8 oz curd cheese (Ricotta)	
3 egg yolks	
Salt, pepper, nutmeg to taste	
2 oz grated parmesan	

Remove the stalks and wash 2 lbs spinach. Drain and cook in boiling salted water. When the water reboils, drain the spinach. Run cold water over it and press very dry with the hands. Chop finely and put in a saucepan with rest of ingredients. Stir briskly for a minute or two and allow to cool.

When cold roll into small sausages (2″ long). Flour them and lower into boiling salted water (6 or 8 at a time). Simmer and as they rise remove them.

Lastly pour over melted butter and sprinkle with parmesan and serve.

Arnold Machin

R.A. 1956

Born: 1911. Studied: Stoke School Art; Derby School Art; RCA.
Silver medal and Travelling Scholarship for Sculpture, 194). Designed new coin effigy,
1964, 1967 (decimal coinage); definitive issues of postage stamp, 1967;
Silver Jubilee Crown. O.B.E. 1965.

You will see that this recipe does not contain meat and this is because as a family we do not eat meat.

I thought that Stuffed Marrow, which we always have at Christmas, might be of particular interest because our meat eating friends are always rather concerned as to "how we manage at Christmas."

Stuffed Marrow is, in fact, known as 'The Bird' in our family because our son, when very young and intrigued by the veneration shown to turkeys at Christmas by other families (where one of the major problems of that festival often seemed to be whether or not "the bird would go in the oven"), gave it that name which has remained with it ever since.

The rest of our meal at Christmas is much the same as other people's except that where suet and lard is used in mince pies and puddings we replace it with vegetable margarine or butter.

Stuffed Marrow

1 large marrow
Butter or margarine
Mushrooms
Parsnips
Carrots
Potatoes
The stuffing
Onions
Garlic
Mixed herbs
Breadcrumbs (3 cups)
Grated cheddar cheese (1 cup)
3 eggs

Peel and remove the top of a large marrow. Spoon out the pips and fill up to ⅔rds of the marrow with stuffing (which will swell and completely fill it when cooked), replace the top, spread with butter or margarine and wrap in foil.

Cook it until it is soft in a hot oven, then remove the foil and allow it to brown.

When it is ready put it on a very large dish and arrange fried mushrooms all down the length of the marrow and surround it with parsnips and carrots which have been cooked in foil, and potatoes which have been baked in butter or margarine until they are crisp. With this serve also a dish of brussel sprouts mixed with boiled shelled chestnuts, gravy flavoured with onion and herbs and home-made horseradish sauce.

The stuffing

Fry four or five large chopped onions and some garlic. Add plenty of mixed fresh herbs such as sage, thyme, parsley and marjoram. Add breadcrumbs and cheese, stirring all the time.

Remove the pan from heat and beat in eggs.

Donald Hamilton Fraser

A.R.A. 1975

Born in London of Scottish parents 1929. 1949-52 Studied at St Martin's School of Art, London; 1953-54 Studied in Paris with a French Government Scholarship, 1958 Tutor in School of Painting at the Royal College of Art, London; 1969 Fellow of the Royal College; Honorary Secretary of the Artists' General Benevolent Institution.

I became a vegetarian years ago, not from an ethical position but simply as part of some medical treatment that I was having. Although I would never dream of changing now, I am not a very good example as I have been known to eat a little meat once in a blue moon so as not to be a damned nuisance or offend some kind person. But it is 99.9% and my wife has long since joined me and risen to the occasion by becoming a marvellous vegetarian cook.

The only problem is that it is all so delicious that I tend to get fat particularly on Judy's wholemeal fruit cakes, rice dumplings filled with mozarella cheese, ratatouille quiche and a splendid *dhal* that she makes from a favourite recipe of her grandfather's who was in the Indian army and probably lived on the stuff.

As I have very simple tastes, finding nice non-meat food while travelling presents no problem and, in fact, is rather fun. There are things like the *tarte aux poireaux* with a bottle of Chablis at Andre in Paris, *zdorovie* salad in a crisp potato shell and vegetable *piroshki* taken with vodka at the Astoria in Leningrad or, in Zurich, the muesli and cream smothered in fresh berries. Nearer home, I never miss a chance to eat at Hendersons in Edinburgh, arguably the best vegetarian restaurant in Europe. Recently I have spent a bit of time in and around Jerusalem where it is particularly easy to be a vegetarian. Wonderful fruit and vegetables, *falafel* from the stalls of the Jaffa Road and the Damascus gate, a very remarkable mushroom canneloni at the King David. I remember one glorious hot day in Jericho last year and a lunch of humus, half a dozen different spicy salads, hot *pita* bread and lashings of a very cold Maccabee beer. Oh yes, vegetarians do enjoy their food.

Ratatouille Quiche

8 oz wholewheat self-raising flour
4 oz best margarine
1 small onion
1 clove of garlic
1 courgette
1 small aubergine
1 green or red pepper
2 tblsp olive oil
4 oz cheddar cheese (strong)
3 eggs
7 fl oz milk
Salt and pepper
2 tomatoes

Grate cheese into eggs and milk, and whisk together well. Season. Place cooled ratatouille into pastry shell and pour on beaten egg mixture to almost fill the pastry shell. Thinly slice the two tomatoes and arrange on the top. Return to oven and bake for 30 minutes or until filling is set and golden (gas 5, or 375°C). Serve hot or cold with tossed green salad.

To make ratatouille Peel and finely chop onion, crush garlic clove, slice courgette, aubergine and pepper (having removed seeds). Fry all the vegetables in the olive oil for 5-10 minutes until they are tender. Allow to cool.

For pastry shell Rub margarine into flour until it resembles fine breadcrumbs. Stir in enough cold water to form dough, roll out and line a 8-9 inch flan dish. Bake blind in a pre-heated oven (gas mark 5 or 375°) for about 10 mins. Remove.

Philip Sutton

A.R.A. 1977

Born: 1928. Studied: Slade School. Awarded Slade Summer Composition Prize 1952
and French State Scholarship. Member of the London Group 1956.
Taught: Slade School, 1955-81. Lived temporarily in Fiji Islands.

I think that food and painting are all that life is about. Eating is quite as important as painting. I'm very conscious about what I eat.

I can roast chicken and do chops but I'm not a cook. I come from a Jewish background and food is a very important part of being a Jew. I work very hard and when I come down from the studio, I could eat anything, I'm so hungry. I am not sophisticated about eating.

I do a lot of running and swimming and my food is mainly related to my sports activities. I start the day by going to the swimming pool and swim for 45 minutes every morning. Then I come back and I have what's called a "health breakfast," muesli which I make myself with sultanas and nuts and fresh fruits. I have a large bowl of this with milk or orange juice and I have two pieces of toast. I work till about half past one and then put on my running shorts and go for an hour's run. When I get back I have an apple and some cheese and coffee. I work till 7.30 come down from the studio and have dinner.

I think the more exercise you take the less food you need. The proteins and vitamins get used up but your body seems to adjust to it. Before I started to take exercise I used to consume numerous cream buns and Mars bars at 11 and in the afternoon. Now I never touch them. What triggered off the exercising? The need to feel healthy. Now I would feel very frustrated without it.

Rebekah
1981 Sutton

Mushroom and Nut Flan

Serves four people

6 oz brown bread

2 oz mixed nuts

2 oz butter

1 clove garlic

1 large onion

½ lb mushrooms

Soy sauce

1 large tomato

2 oz cheddar cheese

Put the bread into a blender to crumb and turn into a flan dish. Grind the nuts in the same way and mix with the bread crumbs. Rub 2 oz butter into the mixture and put under a hot grill to toast for 3 minutes. Moisten with 2 or 3 tablespoons of water and press down to form a flan base.

Melt 2 oz butter in a pan and add the crushed garlic and diced onion. Cook slowly for a few minutes and then add the mushrooms. After about 15 minutes douse with soy sauce and add a few tablespoons of water to increase the juice. Pour this mixture over the flan base. Slice the tomato and arrange on top of the mushrooms. Grate the cheese and sprinkle this on top. Put under a hot grill until brown.

Anne Stonehill
REGISTRY

Frittata

1 large onion

2 good handfuls of fresh spinach

½ oz butter

½ pint milk

1 thick slice white bread (crusts removed)

4 eggs, beaten

2 tblsp grated cheese

Salt and pepper

Finely chop onion, wash and destalk spinach. Melt butter in frying pan, add onion and cook till transparent, then add spinach. Heat milk; add crumbled bread, beaten eggs, cheese, salt and pepper. Add mixture to onion and spinach. Place under grill until brown, turn over and brown other side, serve hot or cold.

Liz Bryant
RESTAURANT MANAGERESS

Vegetables
and
SALADS

Richard Eurich

R.A. 1953

Born 1903. Studied: Bradford School Arts and Crafts; Slade Sch.
Exhibited: NEAC; London Group; R.A. Official war artist.
Representative work in various public galleries.

When I lived in Earl's Court on my own, my staple diet was macaroni cheese, which I learned to make of just the right texture and which warmed, filled and fed me at a low cost.

When I married and went to live in a thatched cottage in the New Forest; economy was still a governing factor. Herrings were 2d each and they figured largely in our diet. For many years the sale of a painting was celebrated by Welsh Rarebit!

During the war, soups of any available vegetables were popular. We had a friend who was a mycologist who used to walk across the heath from Beaulieu to supper. He had an empty paper bag at first, but when he arrived it was bulging with all the fungi he could find and which we wouldn't have dared eat if he hadn't certified them.

Our garden was heathland and wouldn't grow vegetables for some time until we had limed and manured it. Now we grow early potatoes, beans, spinach and lots of herbs of which we are fond.

We still like vegetable soups. We are not vegetarian though two of our three children are.

We like gammon, ham and fish, but vegetarian dishes are very popular. I love a good Stilton. Cooking is not often according to a recipe. If friends admire a dish and want to know how it's made, the answer is often "all the odd bits left in the fridge." We are not teetotalers, but have never indulged in wines, etc. except on very special occasions.

Salad

Chopped red cabbage
Chives
Parsley
Tart apple
Stoned dates
Sultanas
Nuts
Celery
Red pepper
Cooked brown rice
Dressing
Olive oil
Lemon
Salt

Mix together. Serve with a bowl of sliced tomato sprinkled with chopped sweet basil and a dish of grated cheese.

William Scott

A.R.A.1977

Born 1913. Studied: Belfast College of Art; Royal Academy Schools, London.
Worked in Italy and France 1937-39. Work represented in many Galleries in
Great Britain and abroad. A major retrospective exhibition of his paintings and
drawings was held at the Tate Gallery in 1972. C.B.E.1966

I am very absent minded when eating, particularly at Royal Academy Dinners when I never know what I've eaten. It's because I'm completely involved with the people I am speaking to. I have never been able to reconcile eating and talking. I don't know how people manage these business lunches or working breakfasts. I am constantly tapped on the shoulder by waiters to know if I've finished eating.

I go home after these lovely dinners and my wife says "What did you have?" I try to remember to bring the menu home, otherwise I would have no idea.

No, I don't cook. I can boil eggs and make an omlette. I do have a favourite dish and I can make it! It's one you don't often come across in England but all Celtic people enjoy potato cakes. There are Scottish potato cakes and Irish potato cakes, I'm actually half Scottish, half Irish, brought up in Ireland and I go for the Irish version.

We would like to eat out more if we could afford it. When we were young we spent a lot of time in France and got used to going out for meals but it's an expensive habit now. An important point about eating well is the wine – good food is only an excuse for drinking good wine! I think a little discussion about the wines is often enlightening and helps appreciation.

Irish Potato Cakes

½ lb potatoes

2 ozs flour (about)

Salt

Boil the potatoes and mash while still hot. Sprinkle in most of the flour and mix well together. Season with salt. Roll out thin on to a well floured board and cut into wedges. Heat a griddle or large frying pan, test by dusting on a little flour which should brown quickly when hot enough, brush off and cook the cakes about three minutes on each side or until dappled brown.

These can be eaten hot with butter or are delicious fried with bacon.

Sandra Blow

R.A. 1978

Studied: St Martin's; RA Schools; Accademia di Belle Arti, Rome.
Tutor Painting School, RCA 1960-1975. Exhibited: Britain, USA, Italy, Denmark,
France. Works in Tate; Museum of Modern Art, New York; CAS; Walker Art Gallery,
Liverpool; V & A; Fitzwilliam; etc.

I'm a late starter as a cook. For years I did try to disregard all domestic things and just paint. But now quite recently I'm learning to cook.

I used to live quite near to a Cordon Bleu School and I was on the brink of going but I never did and I've regretted it ever since, I might have had a lifetime of Cordon Bleu cooking!

I've just given three dinner parties that were quite successful. Afterwards I make notes. I like to have a first and third course that I can prepare the day before, so I've only one to worry about on the night as I'm inexperienced.

I think timing is important, so that everything is ready at the right moment. Flavour and freshness is important. Food should look good, so should the table. I don't have much silver and linen, anyway it would look absurd in my rather rough working studio. I put great sheets of coloured paper on the table and amongst the real plates have some brilliantly coloured paper plates.

The whole effect is rather like the big collages that I am working on and that are on the walls of the studio.

Angela MacFarlane's Courgettes and Parsley

1 lb small courgettes
2 oz butter
Plenty of chopped parsley
2 oz fresh white breadcrumbs
Salt and pepper

Slice courgettes paper thin. Sprinkle with salt. Leave for a couple of hours in sieve to drip through. Strain and wash off salt. Dry carefully in cloth.

Fry gently in butter (NOT TOO LONG), hardly cook at all – sweat rather than fry.

Put in warm baking dish with butter they were fried in lots of chopped parsley, and breadcrumbs made from fresh white bread. Salt and pepper, be careful with salt as some might remain from salting at commencement. Layer of courgettes, layer of parsley etc, breadcrumbs over final layer.

Put in hot oven reg 7/425° for 15 mins. If with roast for last 15 mins.

Delicious and looks pretty.

Green Salad

Curly Kale – young shoots

Plenty of fresh mint and parsley

Young spinach leaves

Chopped spring onions – including green part

Bits of chopped fresh thyme and rosemary

Mix together and toss in dressing of olive oil, wine vinegar, mustard, salt, pepper, sugar, cinnamon and garlic.

Ann Christopher A.R.A.

Persian Rice

Basmati or patna rice

Butter

Orange peel

Yoghurt or sour cream

Saffron (optional)

Make any quantity, allowing 3 ounces of rice for each person. Use

Basmati or Patna rice (both are fine long-grain rices).

Soak the rice overnight. Boil the rice. Line a dish with butter. Put the rice into the dish with lots of orange peel and bake it. Add a little yoghurt or sour cream (a little saffron too, if you have some) and serve with curry or kebabs.

Maxwell Fry R.A.

Ernö Goldfinger

R.A. 1975

Born 1902 in Budapest. Ecole National et Superieur des Beaux Arts Paris.
Architect & Town Planner. Works: Houses at Le Touquet, Hampstead (own house),
Brussels, Coombe Hill, Windlesham, Amersham etc. Schools at Hammersmith,
Putney, Haggerston. Ministry of Health headquarters Elephant & Castle.
Odeon Cinema, Elephant & Castle. Housing, Abbots Langley, Tower Hamlets,
North Kensington. French Government Tourist Offices, Piccadilly and
127 Avenue des Champs Elysées, Paris.

BREAKFAST
Tea, grapefruit, porridge, kipper – or bacon and eggs – or scrambled
eggs with tomato mixed in.

LUNCH & DINNER
Vegetable soup, RAKOT KRUMPLI (layered potatoes) a Hungarian
dish of sliced boiled potatoes, hardboiled eggs, cream and butter
sprinkled with dried breadcrumbs and baked in the oven.
PULISZKA (polenta Transylvanian style). GULYÁS (Goulash) a
paprika dish of beef, veal, pork or calves' liver. FILLET STEAKS
very underdone, with Béarnaise sauce and chips.
*I like most fish – fish and chips, Jellied eel, truite au bleue, Dover sole
and all crustaceans, caviar, oysters & Japanese raw fish.*

VEGETABLES
Spinach, petits pois à la Française, French beans.
Chinese food – No Greek food.

SWEETS
RICE boiled in milk with vanilla sugar and a nut of butter sprinkled
with grated bitter chocolate (baby food). Austrian cakes – Linzer or
Sacher – Scotch shortbread – French Tarte aux fruits – Millefeuilles.

CHEESE
Best are Roquefort, Reblochon, Brie, Camembert. It is said
there are 365 cheeses in France and a different wine to go with each
– don't ask me which. De Gaulle said "How can one possibly run a
country which has 365 different cheeses."
*I lived in France from 1920 to 1934 and learnt to love French cooking,
the best is between Dijon and Lyons in Burgundy but anywhere
will do. . . .*

DRINKS
With Fish Chablis (too expensive now) or Pouilly Fuissé or Fumé or
Muscadet. With meat red Burgundy. With cheese red Bordeaux
(claret) or Rioja. "Vin Ordinaire" will do for me anywhere in France.
Dry Samos white wine in Greece (not Retsina). The Californian
wines are wonderful, but too expensive even in the U.S.A.
*In Moscow the food in the hotels was awful until we discovered that
for the "food tickets" we could get caviar and vodka so for a week we
lived on this food for the Gods. When we were invited to the
architects' clubs the food was excellent.*

Norman Hepple

R.A. 1961

Born 1908. Studied: Goldsmith's College; R.A. Schools. Figure, subject and portrait painter. Portraits include H.M. The Queen, H.R.H. The Duke of Edinburgh, H.R.H. Prince Charles, H.M. The Sultan of Oman.

The difficulty about sensible eating is that children are brought up thinking of food as a treat or bribe. It's hardly surprising that they spend the rest of their lives indulging themselves.

I have become rather a crank about food. I think I should consider whether what I eat will be harmful, so it's fruit and raw vegetable salad at lunchtime, maybe some yoghurt. We make all our own bread. I like puddings and cakes but they're bad for you.

When I was a boy I had a bad attack of jaundice, and for three weeks I was on a diet of fruit and dry biscuits, and lay in bed reading Mrs Beeton and dreaming of the extravagant meals I'd have when I was better. We don't eat out much now, and I'd probably choose grilled sole and a bottle of good wine – possibly a pudding.

Special Salad

Dates	½ banana
Grapes	Sliced celery
Grated apple	Beanshoots
Carrot	Cabbage finely sliced
Nuts	
Sliced cucumber	

Combine in any quantity and mix with a mayonnaise. (See recipe for mayonnaise, page 155).

Geoffrey Clarke
R.A. 1975

Born: 1924. Studied: RCA. Artist and Sculptor. Won prizes for engraving:
Triennial, 1951; London, 1953; Tokyo, 1957. Commissions: Coventry Cathedral;
Univs of Liverpool, Exeter, Cambridge, Oxford, Manchester and Lancaster.
Works in: Tate, V & A, Museum of Modern Art, New York.

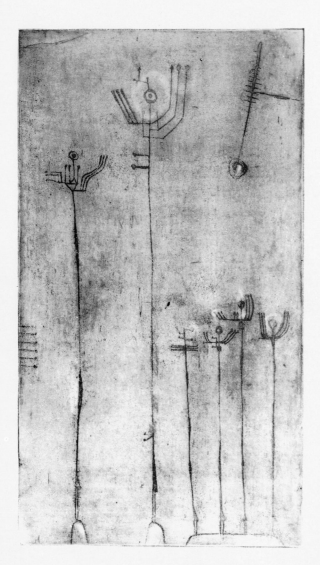

After this budget it is
perhaps fortunate that I have never
developed a palate either fastidious
or expensive to satisfy. As I
invariably tend towards excess of
whatever, I consider it something of
a blessing under present circum-
stances that I can also do without
alcohol. (Unfortunately, the same
does not apply to tobacco).

I'm sorry but 'progress'
cannot fail to increase the number
of beans and chips members.

Pease Pudding

Liquor from boiling bacon or gammon

1 lb or ½ kilo yellow split peas

2 or 3 ozs butter

Salt and pepper

    Parcel up the peas in a cotton, or similar, pudding cloth, leaving a little – but not too much room for expansion. (Do not pre-soak the peas.) Bring bacon liquor to the boil and put the peas into the pot. Top up with water and cover completely. Bring back to the boil and simmer very gently for 1½ to 2 hours. Poke the pea bag now and then with the handle of a wooden spoon so as to circulate the liquor.

    Have two receptacles, such as basins ready. Take the pea bag from the cooking pot and place in one of the basins. Pour off any residual liquor from the basin.

Remove the pudding cloth and mash the peas with the butter and add a little salt and pepper to taste.

    Now take about ⅓ to ¼ of the pea mixture and place in a blender with about 1 to 2 tablespoons of the liquid from the pot and blend until smooth then put into the second basin. Do this again with similar quantities of the peas until all have been so treated. Leave in the basin to cool – the mixture should set to a butter like consistency.

    Serve with slices of cold gammon, pickles, tomatoes, salad etc.

    NB. The mixing can be done with a fork in the basin, if you do not have a blender, but the result is nothing like as good.

Terence Miles
SECRETARY, ARTISTS' GENERAL
BENEVOLENT INSTITUTION

Hot Potato Salad

1 lb new potatoes

½ lb frankfurters

2 tblsp of olive oil

1 dessertspoon of lemon juice

small onion

parsley

dijon mustard

salt and pepper

    Cut new potatoes in half and boil. Simmer frankfurters separately. In a large serving bowl, make a dressing with the olive oil, lemon juice, chopped onion and parsley, a good dollop of dijon mustard and plenty of freshly ground black pepper. Add drained potatoes and sliced frankfurters, toss well and serve either hot or cold. (Add more oil if it absorbs 2 tablespoons and still looks quite dry.)

Susan Macadam
TRUST OFFICE

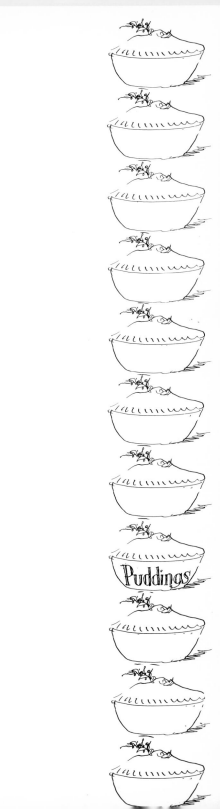

Puddings

John Aldridge

R.A. 1963

Born 1905. Classical Scholar at Corpus Christi, Oxford. No formal art training. First one man exhibition at the Leicester Galleries 1933. Elected ARA 1954. Taught at Slade School 1949-70. Lives in Essex. Work in many public collections including Tate Gallery, Victoria & Albert Museum and the National Portrait Gallery.

I don't have any cranks or fads about food. I always have a good breakfast, eggs and bacon or fishcakes, something like that. We have a cold lunch and have our main meal in the evening. We usually eat in the kitchen even when we have visitors. We have a lovely large country kitchen with an Aga so it's always warm and comfortable. Visitors seem to like it, they wouldn't enjoy being fed in the dining room nearly so much. A birthday treat? Oh, salmon, but we'd have it at home not in a restaurant. We have wine every evening, just plonk but we always have some.

The most memorable meals I remember were those lunches prepared by Mrs. Hubbocks (the Royal Academy's Housekeeper during the 1950s) for members of the Selection and Hanging Committees.

They were marvellous – sometimes hot, and sometimes cold, lovely dishes of beef and pies and cheeses.

The beef was always served with a superb Horseradish sauce about which, amongst other culinary delights, I used to tell my wife. She was full of wonder about someone who could do that sauce for such a lot of people herself having wept torrents of tears grating horseradish for 3 or 4 people.

On the first Ladies' Night I took her to the Academy for dinner and there was Mr. Hubbocks. Instantly she asked him how his wife made the Horseradish sauce I had so much praise for. "Of course, it's delicious," he said, "we only use the best – Frank Cooper's with good fresh cream"!

Meringue, Brandy and Chocolate Pudding

12 Meringue shells
½ pt. cream
1 miniature bottle of brandy
4 oz Terry's bitter chocolate

Make Meringues with 4 egg whites and 8 oz sugar in the ordinary way or buy them in a box which will have no ill effect. Beat the cream until the whisk leaves a trace on the bowl, add the brandy bit by bit and beat until the mixture just holds shape. Break 6 Meringue shells evenly into an oblong freezer container (roughly 10″ by 4″), spread cream and brandy mixture on top, break the rest of the Meringues over the cream and press down lightly. Cover with lid of the box and freeze until wanted (from 6 hours to a week or more). An hour before serving turn the Meringue block out onto a dish (don't worry about crumbs falling about) and cover with a bitter chocolate sauce made by melting the chocolate in a tablespoon or two of water over a low flame. The consistency should be that of thick cream. It will set immediately on the ice cold pudding of which the most hardened pudding haters always want a second helping – in my experience.

Caramel Custard

Ingredients:

For the Caramel: 4 oz sugar, ⅓ pt. water, pinch of cream of tartar.

For the Custard: 2 oz sugar, 3-4 eggs and 1 egg yolk. 1 pt. milk, 1 vanilla pod.

A light caramel custard is ideal to follow the chicken & white wine casserole (see page 80).

To make Caramel: Put sugar, water and cream of tartar into a small saucepan and bring to boil over very high heat. Boil until mixture turns a dark golden colour and pour quickly into a 1½ pt. – 1 quart soufflé dish (or oven-proof porcelain mould) tipping the dish gently to cover the base, and if possible the sides. The area covered will depend upon the consistency of the caramel which is sometimes difficult to control.

Two words of warning:

1) Be careful not to let the caramel burn and

2) Do not let the caramel come into contact with bare flesh as it will be well over 300°F. <u>Do not be tempted to lick the spoon</u>. Put dish aside.

To make Custard: Whisk the eggs and the extra yolk together with the sugar in a large bowl.

Heat the milk (do not boil) with the vanilla pod and pour into egg mixture. (Having first removed the pod from the milk). Now pour this custard through a fine sieve into the caramel lined dish.

Stand in a baking tin containing boiling water and bake for 1 hour in a pre-heated oven 325°F./Reg. 3. Test by inserting a knife into the custard, if cooked the knife will emerge quite clean. Remove from the oven and place immediately in refrigerator. If required in the evening this dish is best made in the early morning.

To turn out the custard. About an hour before serving loosen the edges with a knife and stand dish in boiling water for a few seconds, remove, place serving dish over the mould and quickly turn upside down. The caramel custard should slip easily from the mould. A flat bottomed serving dish with ½inch or so vertical sides is necessary as the caramel will be liquid and far too tasty to lose.

Peter Coker R.A.

Robert Buhler

R.A. 1956

Born 1916. Studied: St Martin's; Zurich and Basle. Exhibited: London Group;
NEAC and London galleries. Works in Tate; V & A; New Zealand and Canada.
Member of London Group. Taught at RCA, Chelsea and Central School.
Portraits include: Dame Edith Evans, Francis Bacon, Stephen Spender,
Sir John Betjeman.

DAME ETHEL WALKER PAINTING HER LUNCH —
— AND WHAT SHE HAD FOR AFTERS:
COLD LEMON SOUFFLÉ

EGGS LEMONS GRATER SUGAR BOWL & WHISK SOUFFLÉ DISH

Cold Lemon Soufflé

6 oz curd cheese

2 eggs

1-2 lemons

sugar to taste

Put cheese in bowl, stir in yolks – one at a time, add juice of lemons and finely grated rinds of 1½-2 lemons. Add granulated sugar to taste. Whisk whites of eggs until stiff, and fold in. Serve in individual soufflé dishes and prepare at least 3 hours before eating. Keep in refrigerator.

David McFall

R.A. 1963

Born: 1919. Studied: RCA; Birmingham and Lambeth Art Schools. Sculptor.
Numerous official commissions including many portrait busts: HRH Prince Charles;
bronze figure of Sir Winston Churchill.

I'm a Sunday cook! My wife gets very little pleasure out of cooking, she cooks out of duty and she hates shopping, so I fill in the gaps. I'll do Sunday lunch and I always do breakfast.

I don't think sculptors are better cooks than painters. I remember Epstein saying to me in Paris that the way to find Brancusi's studio was to follow the empty yoghurt cartons. When we asked him about living on yoghurt, he said: "I've given it up, I had such stomach troubles. I just have hot water now." He was a very old man then. Epstein couldn't cook, he couldn't even make a cup of tea. I worked in his studio on and off for 13 years. He once brought down a 7th Dynasty Egyptian carving, a sacred monkey in porphyry. I was speechless with astonishment to think that I could hold it in my hand – I couldn't make a suitable remark. Soon afterwards lunch was served and when I saw that I let out a yell of enthusiasm. "Ah!" said Epstein "some reaction at last!"

I've tried to diet all my life, everyone tells me I'm overweight. I get thrown into an automatic depression if I haven't eaten enough, it's as if my natural salts had drained through a hole in the basement – I simply have to eat. It's compulsive.

We entertain at home, my wife makes a terrific effort on those occasions. She has one or two 'star' dishes and she spends the entire day in preparations. She's very good on cold dishes and on souffles. If we have salad, I'd do the vinaigrette, that's my thing. I love puddings and sweet things. I'm very faddy about keeping saucepans separate, milk for milk and so on. I hate coffee in a tea cup! As a sculptor, I like to use the right tools for the right job.

Crème de Marron

1 large tin marrons in water
½ lb unsalted butter, softened
¼ pint double cream, whipped (or more)

Crush a large tin of drained chestnuts, mix with ½ lb of softened butter and beat to a cream. Chill and serve with whipped cream.

Gumboot Cookery

Tie a piece of towelling
round your neck. Button up
a big mack. Don't put on a hat
– you can have a slow hair
wash in rain water while you
are looking for the mushrooms.
Grab a large basket and a knife
and, before dawn or after a great
rain storm, head for the hills. Tread
softly, for there are skylarks and chalk
blues underfoot and the wind will blow
you to where the sheep paths run. Give a
loud halloo. Watch a fox run up the hill and
where he stops to listen again look carefully.
The flat stones are white like sheep on the
green hills but some gleam softly and shine
like stars. Start to run down into
the valley, for here are your mushrooms. Cut the stems carefully with
a knife and leave the tiny ones for
tomorrow – or someone else. Run home
before your children wake, take off your
gumboots and dry your hair, fry the but-
tons in butter with bacon and scrambled
egg for breakfast. Gosh, I'm making myself hungry. Why have we
always run out of bread? Keep some
brown flat ones for supper. Put a knob
of butter on each. Cover with grated
cheese and grill. An American dish. Before
the sun goes down, put on some trousers
over your bikini and your gumboots and walk
with your back to the sun in among the
blackberry bushes. In this way you will
brown your back and also be able to see
the blackberries. Have you ever got lost in
a blackberry bush trying to pick blackberries
walking towards the setting sun? Do not fear
that you will be followed. I have yet to see anybody following anybody through a lot of
blackberry bushes – it is just not worth it.
When we are tired of blackberries, sugar and
cream, I get around to making Blackberry Water Ice.

Jean Cooke

R.A. 1972

Born 1927. Painter, sculptor and potter. Studied: Central School;
Goldsmith's College; Camberwell; City and Guilds; RC.
Lecturer RC. Work in: RA; RCA; Tate.

If I cook, I don't paint. When I was pregnant I used to make an excuse and say I couldn't stand so we had baked beans, baked potatoes and chops.

We had them for about six years, then I thought 'this is awful' and I tried to change the regime, but the family didn't like change, they liked what they were used to, so it's been hard work, trying to introduce new things.

My father was a grocer and when I was little I used to sit under the counter and eat dog biscuits and crystalized violets and if I wanted something more exotic, I used to put my finger in the drawers of spices. I adored dog biscuits.

Blackberry Water Ice

1 lb blackberries, sieved	
¼ lb sugar	
¼ pint of water	
If possible 2 or 3 sweet scented geranium leaves	

Make a syrup by boiling the sugar and water together for 5 or 6 minutes, with 2 sweet scented geranium leaves. When cool add the syrup to the sieved blackberries, and put into the freezing tray with a fresh scented geranium leaf on the top. Cover with foil and freeze at the normal temperature for ice-making for 2½ hours. A tablespoon or two of rose water makes a fair substitute for the sweet scented geranium leaves. I have never got any geranium leaves or rose water, but we made blackberry water ice every day the summer before last when the sun was so hot and the blackberries were early. It is the cheapest exotic sweet I know.

More Gumboot Cookery If you have got your mushrooms and the tide is out and there is sand, wade out with your shrimping net and catch some shrimps. Make a risotto with shrimps and mushrooms and an onion, tomato and rice. Also fantastically economical.

Next Day Find a fisherman with too many mackerel. Cut and bake with tomatoes. The mackerel, not the fisherman.

'Headrest and handstand'   H. A. Freeth

Andrew Freeth

R.A. 1965

Born 1912. Studied Birmingham College of Art. Rome Scholarship for engraving.
British School at Rome. On staff at St Martin's School for 32 years.
Portrait painter and engraver. Official war artist. Amongst best known works:
Portrait of J Enoch Powell, Sir Alec Douglas-Home, W Somerset Maugham,
G E Moore and Anthony Eden. Elected to the Academy 1955. He is a past President
of the Royal Society of Painters in Watercolour. His landscapes are made up of broad
direct washes of watercolour and body colour.
Teaches at Sir John Cass College.

Food is definitely a pleasure. No, I don't really cook, my wife is very good at it, so I just wash up.

For breakfast we have coffee and toast and honey. I think honey is good for migraine, so I always have it.

We have a cold lunch, beef or ham, something like that. We entertain at home but we'd eat out as a treat. What sort

of meal would I choose? Italian or French, a soup, perhaps Boeuf Stroganoff and what I'm *really* waiting for – the sweet! Probably crème caramel or cheese cake with blackcurrant jam on top, or even icecream or eclairs – though I'm on a no sugar diet!

Food fads? I don't like cheese. I never drink wine now, that's doctor's orders, not inclination.

Summer Pudding

Several slices white bread

1½-2 lbs blackcurrants, raspberries, blackberries or rhubarb

6-8 ounces sugar

Cook the fruit with the sugar and two or three tablespoons of water until just tender.

Line a greased basin (preferably a pyrex or glass one) with slices of white bread which must be fitted close together having taken the crusts off. Pour in stewed fruit – blackcurrant is best – to half fill the basin. Put in a round of bread and then fill up with more fruit. Cover with bread. Make sure the juice has properly soaked the bread by looking all round and at the bottom of the bowl.

Place a saucer over the top with a weight on it and leave to stand in the fridge until the next day. Turn out and serve with cream or custard.

Jubilee Pudding

pint of milk

2 eggs plus 1 egg yolk

sugar

strawberry jam

whipped cream

grated chocolate

Make a baked custard in the usual way, using the milk, two whole eggs and one yolk, and add a little sugar to taste.

Bake until just set: not too firm. Cool.

When cold, spread thinly with the strawberry jam, cover with whipped cream slightly sweetened and then sprinkle all over with grated dark chocolate.

This pudding was invented at the time of Queen Victoria's Jubilee and is usually very popular even with people who do not like custard!

Very Revd. W.P. Baddeley
FORMER CHAPLAIN

Flambé Dates

Black Dates

Almonds

Pistachios

¼ lb butter

1 glass of rum

cane sugar

finely grated orange peel

Peel, slightly incise and stone the dates and replace each stone

with an almond and a pistachio.

Melt the butter in a frying pan and fry dates on low heat. Powder with cane sugar and orange peel. Allow to caramelise slightly.

Pour the rum over the dates and bring to the boil. Remove from cooker and light with a match. Serve and eat as soon as flames die out.

Marie Valsamidi
ASSISTANT LIBRARIAN

Crème Brûlée

4 egg yolks

2 oz caster sugar

½ pint double cream

½ pint single cream

few drops of vanilla

Blend yolks with caster sugar. Pour in the cream, add vanilla and mix well.

Strain mixture into ovenproof dish and cook in bain marie at 350°F./mark 4 for 45 mins to 1 hour until almost set. Chill overnight in the fridge. Two hours before serving sprinkle the top with caster sugar, brown under the grill. Put back in the fridge. Serve with fresh raspberries or strawberries. Serves 4.

Liz Bryant
RESTAURANT MANAGERESS

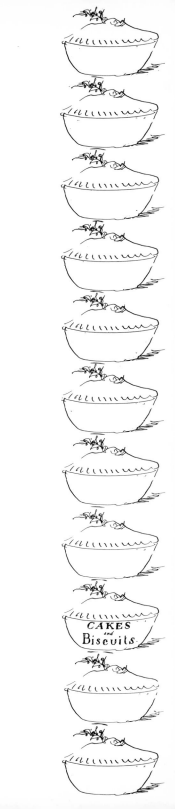

CAKES
and
Biscuits

Ben Levene

A.R.A. 1975

Born: 1938. Studied: Slade; Boise Scholarship 1961-62. Part time teacher
Camberwell School Art. Lived in Spain.

My very special favourite is the chocolate cake. We have it once a year for my birthday. It's very extravagant and really fattening. I like a lot of variety and cheap everyday things. Also meals that are exotic. One thing that's very delicate but very easy to cook is a leg of lamb done in a casserole with butter and mushrooms and garlic and cooked very slowly. For a treat we'll have a really expensive steak. I suppose I'm a "stew" man, but I sometimes make crème caramel, then of course, I make meringues to use up the egg whites. I buy the meat in our family. I go to a really good butcher, not a cheap one. You get far better cheap cuts from a super butcher than from a cut-price one.

One thing I do prefer is to eat my cheese before the sweet. I find that it gets in the way of the tastebuds so I like to keep the savoury things together and build up to the sweet things.

Sacher Torte

Cake

8 oz cooking chocolate (Bourneville best)

8 oz butter

8 eggs, separated

8 oz ground almonds

6 oz caster sugar

1 tblsp corn flour

Filling

8 oz apricots (or 4 oz dried apricots)

sugar to taste

whipped cream to serve

Melt the chocolate with a little water. Cream the butter, add the chocolate, beaten egg yolks, ground almonds and sugar. Beat all ingredients together until very light and creamy. Add cornflour and beat again. Fold in the stiffly beaten egg whites. Transfer gently into a greased 8 inch cake tin and bake in a moderately slow oven 300°/Reg. 2 for 1 hour. Leave in the tin to cool thoroughly before turning out. Meanwhile cook the apricots with sugar and a little water until tender, pass through a sieve. Cut the cake in half, spread the lower half with apricot filling.

Serve with whipped cream.

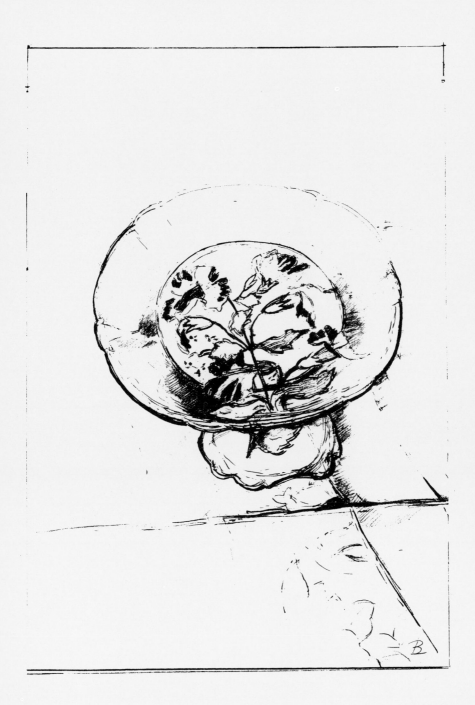

141

Leonard Manasseh

R.A. 1979

Born: 1916. Studied: Cheltenham College; AA School of Architecture.
Won Festival of Britain restaurant competition, 1950. Work: Housing and schools for
local authorities; conservation plan Beaulieu Estate; National Motor Museum
Beaulieu; Wellington Country Park, Stratfield Saye;
Eastbourne Harbour Project.

I cook as rarely as possible – only if obliged to: I'm married to a very good cook. I'm the cook's supervisor! Is cooking creative? O, very much so. It's an art.

I have just a cup of tea for breakfast, unless I'm on a train, then I have the "famous English breakfast." For lunch I have a snack – soup and an avocado pear, nearly always.

We usually entertain at home though we sometimes take the family out on their birthdays. The restaurants vary from good French to exotic Malay and West Indian which the children rather go for. I lived in Singapore for a bit and one of the few puddings I like is Malayan. Gulamalacca it's called; very fine sago in a mould rather like a jelly with coconut milk and molasses. It sounds disgusting but is absolutely delicious. Apart from that my wife makes the most lovely chocolate cake, very rich and made with walnut flour.

I go to a little Italian place where they do calves liver fried very quickly in butter. I'm not sure how they do it, it doesn't taste quite the same at home. It's marvellous.

I have one or two odd tastes, instead of morning coffee I have marmite and milk. It revolts my office but I love it, I think I must need all those vitamins! I've liked marmite ever since I was eight years old – marmite and mustard on hot buttered toast is marvellous! I don't like fruit in green salads and prefer China to Indian tea. I love Lapsang Souchong.

Sarah Manasseh's Chocolate Walnut Cake

3 eggs, separated
3½ ozs sugar
grated rind of ½ orange
1 tblsp orange juice
4 ozs ground walnuts
2 tblsps semolina
¼ tsp baking powder
chocolate butter icing
8″-9″ dia. deep tin

Beat egg yolks and sugar until thick and about twice volume. Add grated orange rind and juice (this makes the cake moist). Stir in finely grated walnuts (finest plate of Mouli vegetable grinder), semolina and baking powder. Fold in stiffly beaten egg whites. Turn into greased and paper-lined cake tin and bake Reg. 4, 350°F for 35-40 mins, until firm to touch and skewer comes out clean. When cold, split in half, put slightly less than half the chocolate butter icing inside and the rest over the top. Coffee icing can be used. Freezes well. Keeps well in the tin in a cold temperature – for about 4 days or so.

Chocolate Butter Icing

4 ozs unsalted butter
approx. 8 ozs icing sugar
2 tblsps cocoa
boiling water

Cream butter, adding sieved icing sugar gradually. As mixture begins to stiffen, add sieved cocoa. Slowly add boiling water to cocoa to make paste, before working into creamed mixture. Continue adding sugar and only add sufficient water to make icing easy to spread. Pull icing over edges to cover sides. However thinly, this helps keep cake moist inside.

Decorate with chopped glacé cherries and walnut pieces and by making patterns with a fork. Any butter cream icing will do.

Olwyn Bowey

R.A. 1975

Born: 1936. Studied: West Hartlepool School Art; RCA. Work purchased for Tate; R.A.;
Ministry of Works; Carlisle Art Gallery. Tutor, Royal Academy Schools.

When I was a student I became a dab hand at cooking meals in one pan. Laziness and never much money mean making good casseroles in winter which last for three days, in one of those lovely iron bottomed dishes which can be heated up on top of the stove and taken to the table. I also make quite good soup which is standard lunch fare. I rarely open tins.

As I can barely be bothered to set a table I welcome summer eating in the garden – usually a quiche, when I can take a slice in one hand and throw away crusts to the dog and dispense with knives and forks. I also read at table, so how beautifully it is set when I'm alone, which is usual, bothers me not at all when there's a book propped up against the bowl of fruit which should grace the centre. One concession I make in my budget is wine which I have only in the evening and I'm fussy about the quality.

I love breakfast, it's my favourite meal of the day. I must have fruit to start with, then I have eggs, boiled or scrambled and toast and marmalade – we make our own (homemade is essential) and real coffee with lots of milk. I get up an hour early just so that I can slump over my large cup of coffee. I write all my letters at breakfast time too.

After I've had half my breakfast, the mood comes over me and I can write letters and all my business, so I spin breakfast out. That's when I feel I can cope with things.

When I became a member of the R.A. I was amazed at the superb lunches served to keep us all going when on the selection and hanging committee for the Summer Exhibition – and along with the Dining Club dinners I feel I get my 'treats' of good food and wine which I enjoy very much, in the nicest way possible – good company, food and wine in a marvellous setting which I never tire of, what more could one want.

Nutties

4 oz granulated sugar
2 oz wholemeal flour
2 oz plain white flour, pinch of salt
1 oz chopped nuts
2 oz dessicated coconut
1 tblsp golden syrup
2 oz butter
½ tsp bicarbonate of soda
1 tblsp hot water

My mother thinks we always ought to have the biscuit jar filled "just in case someone drops in unexpectedly at tea-time." I hope they won't, and then worry that there is nothing to offer when the inevitable happens and I am taken unawares. Therefore I am grateful to her for insisting on making these Nutties – which are the best biscuits ever. People who politely accept one always end up eating half a dozen, and I have seen them

literally sink down in the jar like water in a lock whenever a friends' youngster is present. The dog goes mad for them too.

Preparation

Mix sugar, flours, salt, nuts and coconut in a basin. Melt the syrup and butter together but do not boil. Dissolve the soda in the hot water and mix all the ingredients together. Roll into balls, or put into small rounds with room to expand, on a greased tray. Bake in a moderate oven (350°F)/(180°C) or gas 4 for about 20 minutes. They turn crisp while cooling so its as well to cool them on the trays.

PS. My mother says most people wouldn't try them twice. If they turn out well first time however it encourages you to keep on. I think they're worth any bother (which is I gather taking them out of the oven at exactly the right time and keeping measurements exact) but then I don't make them.

James Fitton

R.A. 1954

Born 1899. Studied: Central School. Member of London Group. Has served on various
panels: Arts Council; RCA Council; Chelsea College Art. Designed
London Transport Underground posters and murals for Festival of Britain.
Illustrations for variety of magazines.

Born and bred high up on the Pennines on the edge of the Yorkshire moors quickly develops the tolerance for a substantial diet as a protection against the bleak northern climate. Steak and Kidney pudding, Suet dumplings, Longjohns and woolly underwear are not just the luxuries that provide comfort and warmth, they are the necessities of existence.

Coming south to the balmy climate of London and to the traumatic experience of marrying a London girl they became just a fond memory and I was re-conditioned for survival. Youghurt, Museli, for breakfast. Salad, Delicatessen, Cheese, Smoked roe, etc. for a very light lunch and a more substantial meal around seven o'clock, preceeded by

the indulgence of a large whisky. A Wesleyan mother's hand reaches out from beyond the grave to restrain and correct the tendency of an unsteady elbow.

My favourite dishes:- Bouillabaise. Fish of almost every kind. Cheese and Onion pie. Wimberry Pie and Pudding. (Wimberries fresh from the moors.) A masochistic liking for Moules Marinière. (I've been poisoned twice by them.)

I like to try new or exotic dishes and I have a most accommodating digestion only rebelling at the nauseous concoctions of chocolate cakes and puddings. In fact I am the ideal dinner guest.

Parkin

8 oz flour	
8 oz medium oatmeal	
a pinch of salt	
2 tsps ground ginger	
½ tsp mixed spice	
½ tsp bicarbonate of soda	
4 oz dripping (fat or margarine)	
8 oz treacle	
4 oz brown sugar	

1 beaten egg

Sieve the dry ingredients into a bowl and mix well.

Melt the dripping, treacle and sugar in a saucepan and stir into the dry ingredients. Add the beaten egg. Pour into a well greased and lined square tin, and bake in a moderate oven (325°F) Reg. 3 for about one hour.

Keep in an airtight tin for a few days until it "comes again."

One Pan Syrup Cake

3 oz butter

4 oz sugar (white or brown)

3 tblsp syrup (or black treacle)

1 egg

¼ pint milk

6 oz s/r flour

1 tsp bicarb. of soda

Melt butter, sugar and syrup, mix in one egg and the milk. Sift flour and bicarb. Add to liquid and beat till smooth. Pour into buttered and floured tin. Bake at 375°F Reg. 5 for ¾ hour or till the centre feels firm.

Variations

a) Add candied peel, or raisins or mixed fruits – about 4 oz.

b) One teaspoon of ginger and some candied ginger.

c) Take out a tablespoon of flour and substitute a tablespoon of cocoa and split when cooked and fill with vanilla butter cream.

I usually make double quantities in a big meat baking tin. Cook at 350°F Reg. 4 for 1¼ hours. It keeps perfectly for up to two months wrapped in cling film and in a tin. The plainer varieties are good sliced and buttered.

Constance – Anne Parker
LIBRARIAN

Orange Cake

2 eggs

Their weight in butter, sugar and flour.

1 tsp baking powder

Finely grated rind and juice of one orange

Icing

4 oz icing sugar

Juice of one orange

Apricot glaze or pureed jam

1 tblsp water or stock syrup

Orange candied peel

Cream butter, beat in sugar until white. Separate eggs. Add yolks one at a time with dessert-spoon of flour and orange rind and juice. Sift remaining flour with baking powder. Whip whites stiffly, fold in with flour. Transfer at once to small cake tin, flatten and hollow slightly on top. Bake in moderate oven 20-30 mins. Turn out and cool. Spread cake with thin layer of glaze or jam. Sieve icing sugar, put in small pan with orange juice and work with water to make thick cream, warm slightly and pour over cake. (It doesn't matter if the icing is slightly runny, as it runs underneath and makes it very goo-ey).

Susan Macadam
TRUST OFFICE

Irish Barm Brack

10 oz sultanas

2 oz mixed peel

7 oz soft brown sugar

¾ pint strained cold tea

10 oz self-raising flour

1 tsp salt

1 tsp nutmeg

1 tsp mixed spices

4 oz margarine

1 cooking apple

1 egg

Put all fruit, except apple into bowl with brown sugar. Pour cold tea over it. Cover and leave to soak overnight. Next day, sieve flour, salt and spices into a bowl. Rub in margarine until like breadcrumbs. Add chopped apple and beaten egg. Pour in the fruit and tea mixture and stir well to make a smooth batter. Turn into a well-lined round 8″ cake tin and bake for about 1½ hours at 180°C, 350°F, Gas Mark 4.

Nicola Figgis
EXHIBITIONS OFFICE

Traditional Polish Kase – Cheesecake

4 oz sweet shortcrust pastry – made with 4 oz flour etc. and 1½ oz caster suger

4 oz unsalted butter, softened

1 lb curd cheese (not cottage cheese)

3 beaten eggs

5 oz caster sugar

3 level dessertspoons cornflour

¼ pint double cream

¼ pint sour cream (optional)

Beat together the butter and the cheese. Add the eggs, sugar, cornflour and double cream and beat the mixture until it is smooth. (The ingredients can be put into a liquidiser and blended until smooth).

Line the base of a greased 8″ cake tin with the pastry. Pour the cheese mixture over the uncooked pastry and bake for 35 to 40 minutes at Gas 5, 375°F, 190°C. Leave the cake to cool in the tin.

Remove the cake from the tin and pour a little of the sour cream over the top. Serve the rest of the sour cream with the cake.

A biscuit base can be used as an alternative to the pastry, but should be cooked before pouring the cheese mixture over it.

This cheesecake freezes well. Serves 6 to 8 people.

Sonia Taylor
FRIENDS OFFICE

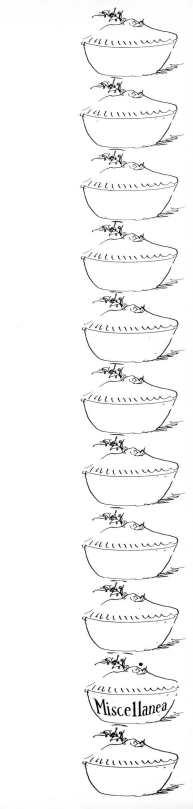

Miscellanea

Frederick Gore

R.A. 1972

Born: 1913. Studied: Ruskin, Westminster and Slade Schools. Head of Painting Dept.,
St Martin's. Works in various public collections. Published: Abstract Art, 1956;
Painting, Some Principles, 1965

At the beginning of the war waiting to be called up, I shared a studio at the top of Constable's House with my sister. She taught in Sidcup so I had to learn to do the cooking. It had a Greek flavour since I had been forced home from Greece by the war. Also there was John Stais, newly established at The White Tower, to give culinary advice as well as interested in paintings of Greece. It was open house in Charlotte Street and I cooked for quite a throng. I was helped by a secondhand cookery book from the Phoenix Library by two ladies (Lyall and Hartley – The Gentle Art of Cooking) who mingled French and Eastern dishes. Munckaczina, an hors d'oeuvre which still pleases and surprises me, is from their section of dishes from the Arabian Nights.

I never mastered British cooking although I continually Bless all good English Puddings and especially Summer Pudding (as eaten by the angels in heaven after long mornings of Tennis or Croquet). Nowadays I hardly cook at all (seeing it as a trap like gardening to destroy painters). But in my household I do prepare mayonnaise and aïoli and sometimes soups. Aïoli is the garlic mayonnaise originally eaten in Provence with boiled salt cod – but now best with any cold fish (especially cod) and meats together with a collection of cold vegetables and of course, potatoes. It is also an ingredient of the fish soup Bourride (Bouillabesse without crustacea) spread on the floating crusts of bread and with the fish itself.

An aïoli d'honneur is the communal village banquet which holidaymakers may join (sometimes it is a pistou when the special dish is a grand mixed vegetable soup liberally flavoured with basil). Beware the pastis and even the 10% wine or you may find yourself afterwards in the arena chased by young bulls or "vachettes" through a mini swim pool.

Aïoli

2-6 cloves of garlic	
2 egg yolks	
olive oil	
salt	
lemon juice	

Six (or at least 2) cloves of garlic crushed in a garlic crusher or pounded in a mortar. Add the yolks of two eggs, mix well and add the olive oil bit by bit, as for mayonnaise. When the sauce is very thick, add salt and lemon juice.

Sir Philip Powell

R.A. 1977

Born: 1921. Studied: AA School Architecture (Hons. Diploma). Works include:
Churchill Gardens flats, Westminster, 1948-62, and many other commissions in
Britain. Won numerous medals and awards for architectural work, including
Royal Gold Medal for Architecture, RIBA, 1974.
O.B.E. 1957 Kt. 1975

Cooking is one of the senior arts but I do it badly and seldom. What I would choose as a favourite meal? Oh, probably an hors d'oeuvre, perhaps hot and odd (Greek or Spanish?) followed by a fish dish with an exciting sauce (French).

After that, I haven't much room left for what is called the main course; but cheese, yes (English), puddings, no.

I like wine very much but there are many times, certainly in the middle of the day, when I wish I were allowed to choose beer. Before a meal I'd much rather have a glass of draught beer or dry sherry than a glass of plonk.

I can't bear currants and sultanas. I remember being made to eat them at a disagreeable prep school; a humane master who couldn't break the rules imaginatively allowed me to have mustard with them. Unlike Joyce's Leopold Bloom I don't eat with relish the inner organs of beasts and fowls – except in pâtés.

A favourite recipe? Don't know – I prefer not to analyse the chemistry of what I'm eating. I enjoy the expectation and surprise.

Mustard Sauce

1 portion English Mustard	
1 portion vinegar	
2 to 3 portions white sugar	

Bring to toothpaste consistancy; don't add anything else. For hot sausages or cold pork.

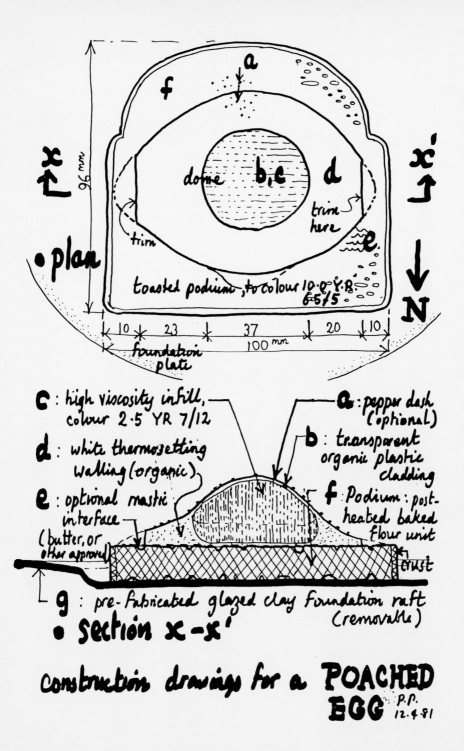

plan

x → x′

96 mm

f

a

dome   b,c   d

trim

trim here

e

toasted podium, to colour 10·0 YR 6·5/5

N ↓

| 10 | 23 | 37 | 20 | 10 |

100 mm

foundation plate

c: high viscosity infill, colour 2·5 YR 7/12

d: white thermosetting walling (organic)

e: optional mastic interface (butter, or other approved)

a: pepper dash (optional)

b: transparent organic plastic cladding

f: Podium: post-heated baked flour unit

crust

g: pre-fabricated glazed clay foundation raft (removable)

● section x-x′

Construction drawings for a **POACHED EGG**

P.P.
12.4.81

Michael Rothenstein

A.R.A. 1977

Born: 1908. Studied: Chelsea Polytechnic; Central School. Works mainly in
water-colour and various forms of graphics, particularly woodcut and silkscreen.
Exhibited internationally and represented in many public collections including:
Tate Gallery; V & A Museum; Museum Modern Art, New York.

"The Right Stuff"*
About eating; about recipes and meals: it was years before I found the "right stuff."

For years, until I was fifty perhaps, I saw the body as a poor old Donkey, and never bothered much about what I gave it to eat. Then, on a visit to America, where reaction against junk food makes people actively diet-conscious, I came across various books about proper eating; books such as Roger Williams' "Nutrition Against Disease," so, at last, I discovered the right stuff. This meant further reading and extracting some working principles that fitted one's own situation: country shopping and limited cooking capacity.

In food preparation I'm a one-finger typist. Various salads and fresh fruit are supported mainly by omelettes, steaks, steamed vegetables. Only at weekends when my busy wife joins me does variety and expertise invade the kitchen.

Breakfast is a meal that is very much under one's own control – unlike the lunches and dinners often eaten away. For the last fifteen years I have breakfasted off all the recommended things, fruit, wheatgerm, lecithin, yoghurt etc. I only eat these excellent things after forty-five minutes of exercise and jogging, but this has made such an extraordinary difference to one's health and energy I don't hesitate to make this rather personal confession!

*With apologies to Tom Wolfe.

A Breakfast Recipe

Two dessertspoons wheatgerm with yeast
Two dessertspoons Lanes Lecithin grains
Three dessertspoons home-made yoghurt
One dessertspoon crunchy muesli
One chopped apple
One dessertspoon Ribena
Small quantity of skimmed milk
Mix everything together

154

Homemade Healthfood

Serves 2-3

5 tablespoons ground nuts

5 dessertspoons bran

1 apple

Demerara sugar

Milk

    Mix ground nuts of all kinds with the bran and a grated apple. Add demerara sugar to taste and eat with milk.

Norman Hepple R.A.

Mayonnaise

2 eggs

2 lemons

¼ pint of sunflower oil

Salt and pepper

    Separate the eggs and put the yolks in a bowl. Beat them with the juice of half a lemon and a little salt and pepper. Gradually add the oil, drop by drop at first and then more quickly as it thickens. Add the rest of the lemon juice, to make a very sharp lemony dressing. Serve with Special Salad.(pp126)

Norman Hepple R.A.

David Tindle

R.A. 1979

Born: 1932. Worked as scene painter and commercial artist, 1946-51. Exhibitions in many public and private galleries in Britain and abroad. Set of 3 mural decorations for Open Univ., Milton Keynes.

"I don't really go in for cooking. If my wife's away, I help myself from the fridge till it's empty. I like a good breakfast, yoghurt, eggs and bacon and toast, if there's time.

Lunch? We used not to bother with much but since I've been teaching at the Royal College of Art, they have such a good canteen that I've got used to a hot, cooked lunch.

We have simple things at home, stews, apple pies. I don't like "dressed up" foods with lots of sauces. If we go out for a meal, we look for good French cooking. I think a really nice dinner is almost an aphrodisiac. Sweet things? I'm not keen on great slices of chocolate gateaux but I quite like cheesecake.

My favourite meal? Oh, avocado, steak and zabaglione.

As I'm a tempera painter who doesn't cook, how about a recipe for egg tempera?! It's only egg yolk and water, *perfectly edible!*

Simple Egg Tempera

| Egg |
| Water |

Separate the egg, prick one yolk and pour the liquid into a glass. The sac must not get into the yolk. Add a little water to make a thin cream and stir well. Mix with pigment to make a paste. Thin with more water to make a useable consistancy and apply quickly – or it will set like concrete.

Index

Index of contributing Members

Index of recipes

Edward Ardizzone

(Painter, 1900-1979), was a true gourmet but according to his autobiography seems as a child to have had a particularly favourite meal –

At high tea the round table was covered with a white cloth. The first course was often a dish of winkles, which we would eat with the help of a pin. Miss Willis was very partial to winkles so Arthur and I would bring them back from Ipswich for her. I liked them too and I too am partial to them to this day. The winkles were followed by lightly-boiled new-laid eggs and bread and butter and strawberry jam. All this was washed down with strong sweetened tea the colour of red mahogany. I can't remember a meal I enjoyed more.

From a page in "The Young Ardizzone" published by Studio Vista a division of Cassells.